Small Group Qs

Small Group Qs

600 Eye-Opening Questions for Deepening Community and Exploring Scripture

Laurie Polich

A DIVISION OF HARPERCOLLINS*PUBLISHERS*

Small Group Qs
600 Eye-Opening Questions for Deepening Community and Exploring Scripture

Copyright © 2002 by Youth Specialties

Youth Specialties Books, 300 S. Pierce St., El Cajon, CA 92020, are published by Zondervan Publishing House, 5300 Patterson Ave. S.E., Grand Rapids, MI 49530.

Library of Congress Cataloging-in-Publication Data

Polich, Laurie.
  Small group Qs : 600 eye-opening questions for deepening community and exploring Scripture / Laurie Polich.
    p. cm.
  ISBN 0-310-24023-9
  1. Church work with teenagers. 2. Bible study and teaching.
  3. Christian teenagers—Religious life—Miscellanea. 4. Christian teenagers—
  Conduct of life—Miscellanea. I. Title.

BV4447 P565 2002
268'.433—dc21

2001039098

Unless otherwise indicated, all Scripture quotations are taken from the *Holy Bible: New International Version* (North American Edition). Copyright © 1973, 1978, 1984 by International Bible Society. Used by permission of Zondervan Publishing House.

Web site addresses listed in this book were current at the time of publication. Please contact us via e-mail (YS@YouthSpecialties.com) to report URLs that no longer are operational and replacement URLs if available.

Edited by Dave Urbanski and Vicki Newby
Cover and interior design by Left Coast Design

Printed in the United States of America

02 03 04 05 06 07 / / 10 9 8 7 6 5 4 3 2

This book is dedicated to six close friends who have taught me by their lives and through their friendship what it means to "live the question":

Donna Barton
Stacy Sharpe
Krista Hughes
Marlo Oshima
Helen Musick
Vivian McIlraith

(Special thanks to Aaron Babyar and Craig Barton, whose questions helped fuel my creativity.)

Contents

THIS IS A DANGEROUS BOOK!

So don't let the title fool you. *Questions change people*. They unlock secrets and dreams that lie hidden in the heart. That's what makes them so powerful.

Through his questions, Jesus inspired people to receive healing they didn't know they needed, confront struggles they didn't know they had, and expose secrets they didn't know they kept. And he invites us to participate in the same ministry. That's what makes your partnership with this book so exciting.

When I wrote *Help! I'm a Small Group Leader!*, I wanted to offer insights on small group leadership. And while *Small Group Qs* is a sequel of sorts, you won't find more leadership tips inside—just a whole lot of questions. (Isn't that what a small group leader really needs, anyway?)

For some of you, this may be a frustrating book—you'd feel a little more secure if the answers were printed in the back! But don't forget how many times the disciples were left without answers when Jesus asked questions. I'm betting that Jesus must have known his questions had a power of their own. So you can trust that truth as you work your way through this book.

The first section starts off pretty painlessly. It contains three subsections of 50 questions each.

There are **Getting Acquainted** questions for the newly formed (or spontaneously informal) small group. This kind of group can happen in a van, on a trip, or at 3 a.m. during a lock-in. So keep a copy of this section handy. It will serve you well at desperation time! If you have an ongoing small group (or a group that meets more than once), these questions get their best mileage if they're used as icebreakers or discussion starters. They'll also help you begin to build community with your group by prompting kids to share their thoughts and desires.

The **Getting Deeper** questions are designed to take your group through more complex issues. (Hence the title.) This can be scary because you never know what issues or emotions may be stirred. But it can also be wonderful because it may spur healing and change needed so that genuine growth can occur. Reserve these questions for when your group has been at it awhile—and when you're ready for some hard-core honesty and trust.

When you want to find out where your students are spiritually (without being too invasive), check out the **Getting Spiritual** questions. They'll not only help you break the ice with newcomers, they'll also spur some interesting dialogue among the Christians in your group. (And it may open your eyes to some surprising discoveries about *their* faith!) Use these as get-to-know-you questions at a camp or retreat or as find-out-what-theology-you-need-to-teach questions for your group at home.

The next section, **Getting into Topics**, offers a range of questions on six popular youth ministry topics. These can be used on their own as discussion starters or as supplemental questions for your own topical Bible studies. (This is a good time to mention that any of the questions in this book can be reworded, readjusted, or rearranged to suit your group's needs! Or you can copy them and claim them as your own. Plagiarism? Welcome to youth ministry! You have the author's permission.)

The final section contains 15 complete Bible studies from the Old Testament and 15 from the New Testament. I've entitled this section **Getting into the Word**. You'll notice three major kinds of questions in these studies—observation, interpretation, and application. Observation questions take you *to* the text, interpretation questions lead you *from* the text, and application questions help you *live* the text. These sections not only provide 30, ready-made small group studies, they also teach you (by example) how to construct all three kinds of questions.

So that's a brief tour through *Small Group Qs*. Enjoy the ride. And remember—your savior did his finest work through his questions. Perhaps you will, too.

GETTING ACQUAINTED, GETTING DEEPER, GETTING SPIRITUAL

150 Questions

50 GET-TO-KNOW-YOU QUESTIONS FOR NEW OR SHORT-TERM SMALL GROUPS

If you won the lottery, what would you buy first?

If you could spend the afternoon with someone famous, who would you spend it with?

If you could choose between being able to breathe underwater, becoming invisible, or being able to fly, which ability would you choose?

If you could visit any place—real or imaginary—where would you go?

If you could meet any character in any book, whom would you meet?

Q 6

If you could live in the past or in the future, which time period would you choose?

Q 7

If you could relive a time in your life, what time would it be?

Q 8

If you met a genie that could grant you three wishes, what would you wish for?

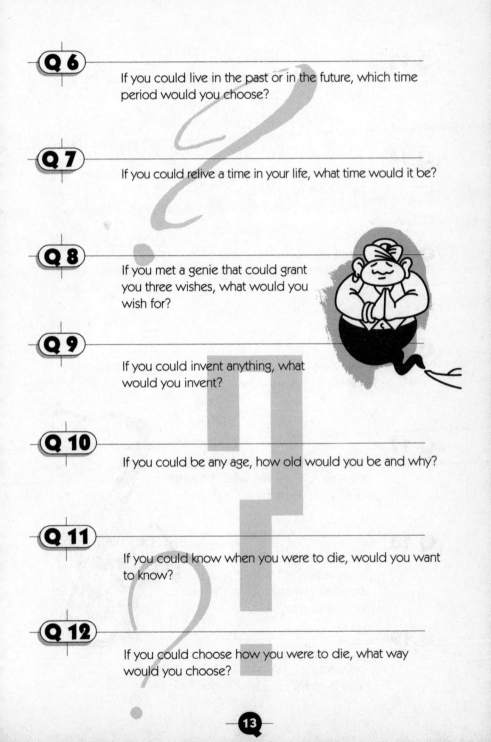

Q 9

If you could invent anything, what would you invent?

Q 10

If you could be any age, how old would you be and why?

Q 11

If you could know when you were to die, would you want to know?

Q 12

If you could choose how you were to die, what way would you choose?

Q 13

If you could only do one thing for the rest of your life, what would you do?

 Q 14

If you could only eat one food for the rest of your life, what would you eat?

 Q 15

If you could be a character in any movie, who would you be?

 Q 16

If your parents let you choose a destination for a family vacation, where would you go?

 Q 17

If you could eat at only one restaurant for the rest of your life, what restaurant would you choose?

 Q 18

If you were able to play any musical instrument with little or no practice, what instrument would you want to play?

Q 19

If you could join any band right now, what band would you join? Would you be the singer or play an instrument? What instrument?

Q 20 If you could be any cartoon character, which character would you be?

Q 21 If you could give up one chore for the rest of your life, which chore would you give up?

Q 22 If you had to watch one movie over and over again for 24 hours straight, what movie would you watch?

Q 23 If you could set your own schedule, what time would you get up in the morning and what time would you go to sleep?

Q 24 If you could cut one class from your schedule, what class would you cut?

Q 25 If you had to teach one subject in school, what subject would you teach?

Q 26 If you could be a professional athlete, what sport would you play?

Q 27

If you could meet a sports star, which one would you want to meet?

Q 28

If you had to change your nationality, what nationality would you become?

Q 29

If someone gave you enough money to open a store, what kind of store would you open?

Q 30

If you could redecorate your room with any theme or design, what would your room look like?

Q 31

If you could be an animal for a day, what animal would you be?

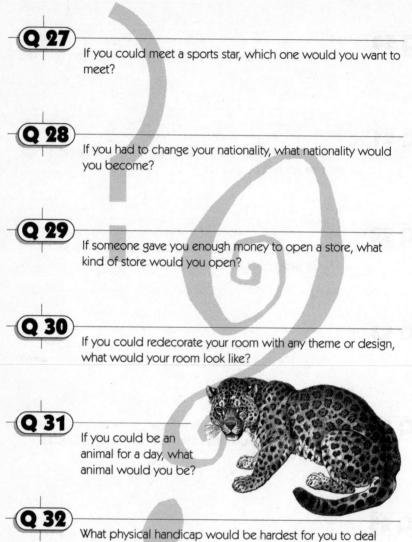

Q 32

What physical handicap would be hardest for you to deal with and why?

Q 33

If you could have lived at any time in history, when would you have lived?

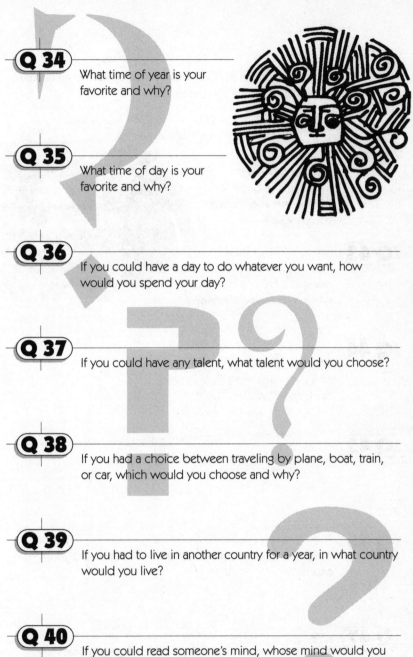

Q 34

What time of year is your favorite and why?

Q 35

What time of day is your favorite and why?

Q 36

If you could have a day to do whatever you want, how would you spend your day?

Q 37

If you could have any talent, what talent would you choose?

Q 38

If you had a choice between traveling by plane, boat, train, or car, which would you choose and why?

Q 39

If you had to live in another country for a year, in what country would you live?

Q 40

If you could read someone's mind, whose mind would you like to read?

If you could be in the *Guinness Book of World Records*, what record would you like to hold?

If you could win the Gold medal in any Olympic event, what event would you choose?

If you had to choose between dying in a fire or a blizzard, which would you choose?

Would you rather be on the cover of *Sports Illustrated*, *Rolling Stone*, or *People*? Why?

What is the strangest food you've ever eaten?

If you had to be allergic to something, what would you choose?

If you could only visit one Web site for the rest of your life, what site would you visit?

Q 48

What are your favorite clothes to wear?

Q 49

If you could choose between spending the day at the beach or in the mountains, where would you spend your day?

Q 50

If your house caught fire and you could choose only one thing to save (besides your family members), what would you save?

50 QUESTIONS THAT INSPIRE INTIMACY—AND TAKE YOUR GROUP TO THE NEXT LEVEL

Q 1

What room in your house best represents your personality and why?

Q 2

If you were stranded on a desert island and could choose only five things to have with you, what would they be?

Q 3

If you could change or improve one quality about yourself, what quality would you alter?

Q 4

If you could have one of your fears or struggles magically taken away, what fear or struggle would you get rid of?

Q 5

If you could go on a vacation with anyone, whom would you invite?

Q 6

If you had to live someone else's life, whose life would you choose?

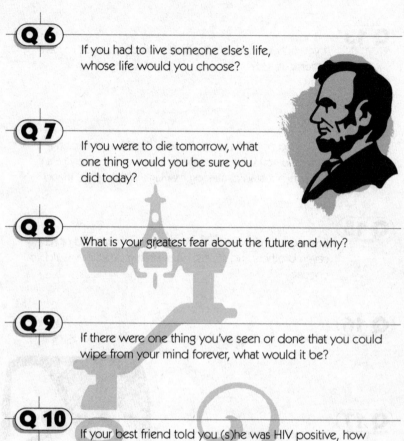

Q 7

If you were to die tomorrow, what one thing would you be sure you did today?

Q 8

What is your greatest fear about the future and why?

Q 9

If there were one thing you've seen or done that you could wipe from your mind forever, what would it be?

Q 10

If your best friend told you (s)he was HIV positive, how would you respond?

Q 11

If you could perform one act of kindness that could make the world a better place, what would it be?

Q 12

If you discovered one of your parents was doing something you knew was wrong, would you confront your mom or dad, tell someone else, or say nothing?

Q 13

If you only lived to be 30, what would you hope to have accomplished?

Q 14

What kind of marriage would you choose—an exciting, 10-year union with someone you love passionately or an average-but-stable, lifelong marriage with a good friend?

Q 15

If you could choose between being an only child or having seven brothers and sisters, what sibling situation would you choose?

Q 16

What was the hardest thing you ever had to apologize for?

Q 17

Was there ever a secret you told and later wished you kept? If so, what was the secret?

Q 18

If you could choose one thing never to deal with again, what one thing would you choose?

Q 19

What season best represents your personality and why?

Q 20

What is the best gift you've ever received—and whom was it from?

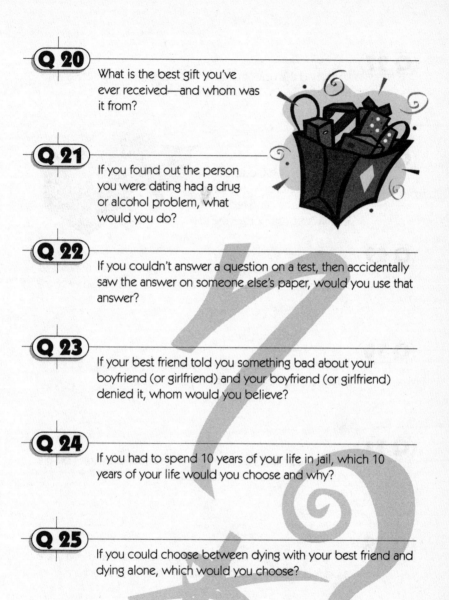

Q 21

If you found out the person you were dating had a drug or alcohol problem, what would you do?

Q 22

If you couldn't answer a question on a test, then accidentally saw the answer on someone else's paper, would you use that answer?

Q 23

If your best friend told you something bad about your boyfriend (or girlfriend) and your boyfriend (or girlfriend) denied it, whom would you believe?

Q 24

If you had to spend 10 years of your life in jail, which 10 years of your life would you choose and why?

Q 25

If you could choose between dying with your best friend and dying alone, which would you choose?

Q 26

If you were on the Titanic when it began sinking, would you get into a life raft or give your place to a stranger?

Q 27

If you had the opportunity to take revenge on someone who hurt you, would you take revenge? Why or why not?

Q 28

If you found $100 outside a 7-Eleven store, would you take the money and report it or would you pocket the cash?

Q 29

If your plane was about to crash, but you had five minutes to write a note, what would you write? Who would you write to?

Q 30

If a friend told you she or he was being physically abused by a family member, how would you respond?

Q 31

If you discovered your parent had read your diary (or a private letter), how would you respond?

Q 32

If a distant relative needed a kidney transplant, and you were a perfect match, would you donate one of your kidneys?

Q 33

If someone told you a secret about your best friend and told you not to tell your friend, would you tell your friend or keep the secret?

Q 34

If you saw two friends cheating on a test, would you say something to the teacher, something to your friends, or nothing at all?

Q 35

If your best friend's boyfriend (or girlfriend) told you he or she had a crush on you, would you tell your friend?

Q 36

If both your parents suddenly died, what person or family member would you want to live with?

Q 37

Of all your family members, whose death would affect you most?

Q 38

If your sister told you she was getting an abortion, would you tell your parents?

Q 39

If you could change one thing about your physical appearance, what one thing would you change?

Q 40

If you and three friends could live on a deserted island forever —with all your needs taken care of—would you choose that life?

Q 41

If your friend's dad was about to drive you and your friend home—but you could tell he had been drinking—what would you do?

Q 42

If your parents were getting a divorce, which parent would you choose to live with?

Q 43

After you die, what is one thing you'd like to be remembered for?

Q 44

If tomorrow were the last day you would ever see your mom, what would you say to her?

Q 45

What has been your biggest accomplishment so far?

Q 46

What is your favorite place to go when you want to get away and think?

Q 47

If you had to name one person who has influenced you the most, what person would you name?

Q 48

Of all your relatives, who are you most like?

Q 49

During what time of day do you feel the most relaxed? The most tense?

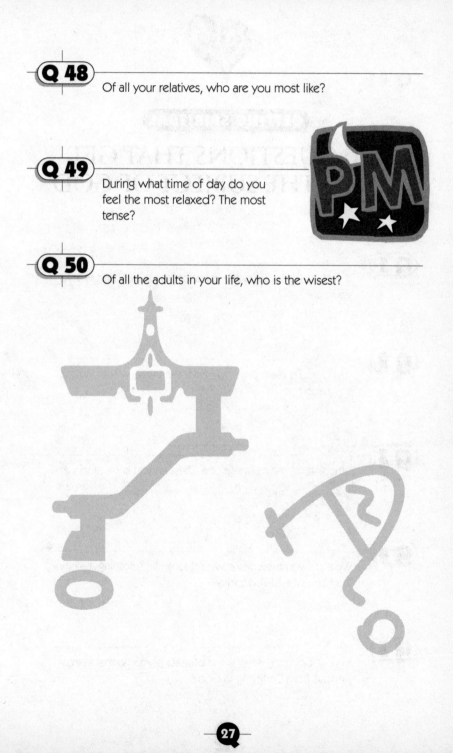

Q 50

Of all the adults in your life, who is the wisest?

50 QUESTIONS THAT GET INTO THE SUBJECT OF GOD

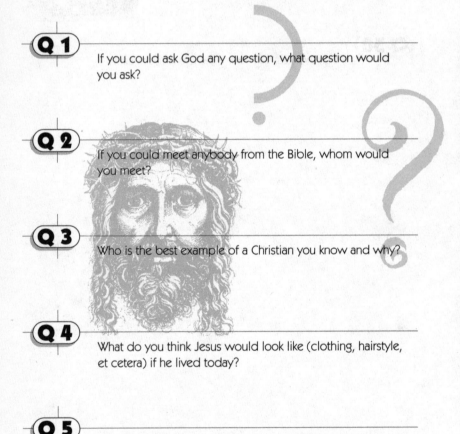

Q1

If you could ask God any question, what question would you ask?

Q2

If you could meet anybody from the Bible, whom would you meet?

Q3

Who is the best example of a Christian you know and why?

Q4

What do you think Jesus would look like (clothing, hairstyle, et cetera) if he lived today?

Q5

In your opinion, what is the biggest obstacle that keeps people from believing in God?

Q 6

Has God ever spoken to you? If so, what was it like?

Q 7

If God agreed to do one thing to prove he exists, what would you want him to do?

Q 8

If Jesus went to your school, what one group would he hang out with most often?

Q 9

Where do you feel closest to God?

Q 10

If Christianity were the only religion that was against the law, would you go to jail or leave the faith?

Q 11

If your pastor stood up one Sunday and said "God is dead," how would you respond?

Q 12

If God is good, why does he allow pain and suffering in the world?

Q 13

Do you believe God loves some people more than others?

 Q 14

If you had to describe heaven, how would you describe it?

 Q 15

Of all the problems of the world, what problem do you think saddens God the most?

 Q 16

If Jesus wanted to hang out with you this Friday night, where would you take him?

 Q 17

If someone asked you to explain the Trinity, how would you describe it?

 Q 18

If there's only one God, why do you suppose there are so many religions?

 Q 19

In your opinion, is there a difference between Mormonism and Christianity?

What parts of the Bible do you have the hardest time believing?

If Jesus came to earth today, where would he live? (e.g., Calcutta? Wichita?)

What do you think happens when you die?

If you fell in love with someone who didn't believe in God, would you consider marrying that person? Why or why not?

If someone were dying and asked you how to know God, what would you tell that person?

Do you ever see God's presence in others? If so, in what ways?

Do you think God is happy with the way he's represented in the world?

Q 27

When do you feel distant from God?

Q 28

If someone said, "I think Jesus was just a good, moral teacher," how would you respond?

Q 29

If someone said, "All religions lead to God," how would you respond?

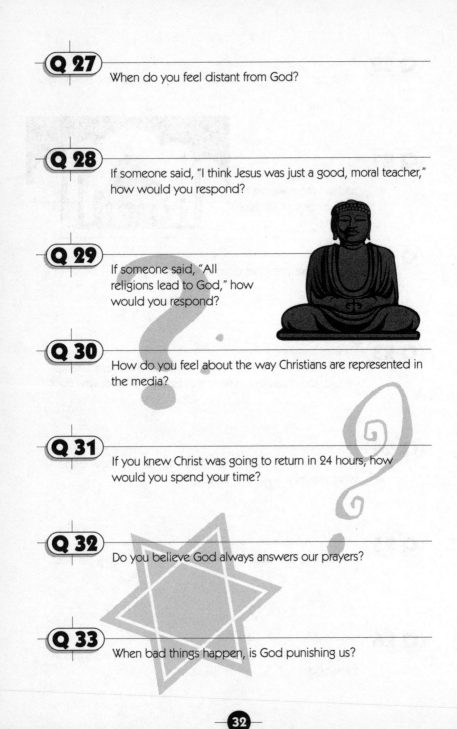

Q 30

How do you feel about the way Christians are represented in the media?

Q 31

If you knew Christ was going to return in 24 hours, how would you spend your time?

Q 32

Do you believe God always answers our prayers?

Q 33

When bad things happen, is God punishing us?

Q 34

Do you believe God is for or against the death penalty?

Q 35

If Jesus went to a voting booth, would he vote as a Republican or Democrat?

Q 36

Do you believe God is pleased with how your parents raised you?

Q 37

If you had one minute on national television to say something about God, what would you say?

Q 38

What do you think it means to "fear God"?

Q 39

If Jesus watched television, what would be his favorite show?

Q 40

What's one show on television that Jesus would never watch?

If Jesus were to follow you around one day, is there anything you'd do differently?

If someone said, "Describe what you think God looks like," how would you describe God physically?

Who's the most spiritual person you know? Why?

Do you feel God's presence more when you're alone or with people? Why?

Do you believe God causes natural disasters (earthquakes, tornados, hurricanes) or do they happen on their own?

How is God's love different from human love?

Do you believe God loves you more when you're good? Why or why not?

If you could advise God to do something differently, what would say?

If someone asked if you knew you were going to heaven, how would you respond?

Would you say you've become more spiritual, less spiritual, or stayed the same over the last five years? Why?

GETTING INTO TOPICS

150 Questions
(25 per topic) on
Self-Image
Friendship
Family Relationships
Love, Sex, and Dating
Missions and Service
Tough Topics

GETTING INTO TOPICS

SELF-IMAGE

Q 1

What do you struggle with the most when it comes to your self-image?
a. Appearance (your looks)
b. Accomplishments (your grades)
c. Status (your popularity)

Q 2

If you could choose between being rich, beautiful, or happy, what would you choose?

Q 3

What personal qualities do you admire most and why?

Q 4

When in your life have you felt the best about yourself? What made you feel that way?

Q 5

When in your life have you felt the worst about yourself? What made you feel that way?

Q 6

Of all your friends, who do you think has the healthiest self-image? Why?

Q 7

Do your parents affect the way you see yourself? If so, how?

Q 8

Have you ever starved yourself or overeaten to make yourself feel better? Did it work?

Q 9

Have you or your friends ever used alcohol to feel better? Did it work?

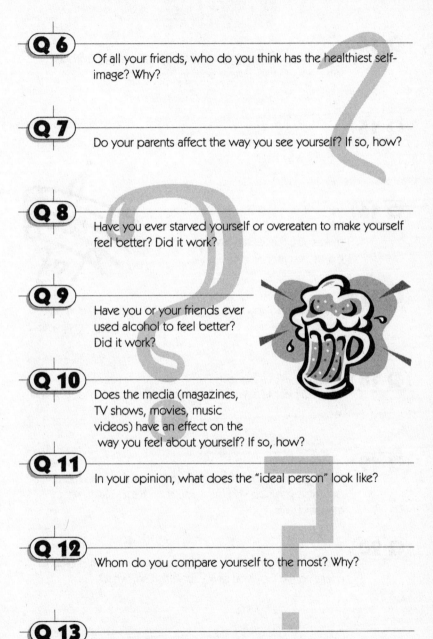

Q 10

Does the media (magazines, TV shows, movies, music videos) have an effect on the way you feel about yourself? If so, how?

Q 11

In your opinion, what does the "ideal person" look like?

Q 12

Whom do you compare yourself to the most? Why?

Q 13

If your mirror had a voice, what would it say when you looked at it?

Do you know people who struggle with eating disorders?
What effect does it have on their self-image?

 Do you think people see themselves the way they really are?
Why or why not?

 When you are depressed, what
makes you feel better? What
makes you feel worse?

 What goals do you have for your life? Will the way you feel
about yourself help or hinder you from achieving those goals?

 What do people at your school do to themselves to look better?

 If you weren't around, how do you think people would
describe you? Do you think you'd be happy with what
they said?

Has anyone ever said something to you that had a profound
effect on the way you saw yourself? If so, what?

A Look at Scripture

For more in-depth Bible studies on self-image, have your group look at the story of the woman at the well (John 4:1-26), Zacchaeus (Luke 19:1-10), and the woman caught in adultery (John 8:1-11). Consider the impact Jesus had on each of their self-images. All three of these Bible stories are given attention in this book—the woman at the well (p. 78), the woman caught in adultery (p. 88), and Zacchaeus (p. 92).

Q 21

Read Psalm 139:13-14. When you think about the way God made you, does verse 14 express the way you feel? Why or why not? According to this psalm, how does the way you feel about yourself mirror the way you feel about God?

Q 22

Look at Proverbs 31:30. According to this verse, what kind of woman is praised? How would you describe the kind of woman who is praised in our world today? Do you think women are valued more for their looks or their character? What effect does this have on their self-image?

Q 23

First Samuel 16:7 describes the qualities we admire in a person and what God admires in a person. What is the difference? If people watched the way you live your life, would they say you're more concerned with your appearance or your heart?

Q 24

Galatians 5:17-24 discusses the differences between our sinful nature and the Spirit of God. As you look at the characteristics of each, which list has more qualities that represent the way you live? When you live out the qualities of your sinful nature, how does your behavior affect the way you feel? When you live out the qualities of God's spirit, how does that affect the way you feel?

Q 25

Jeremiah 29:11 contains a promise to the Israelites that shows God's attention to our lives. What is that promise? When you go through hard times, how could this verse be an encouragement to you? Do you believe this verse shows you are important to God? Why or why not?

GETTING INTO TOPICS

FRIENDSHIP

Q 1

If you had to choose between telling the truth (and hurting your friend) and lying to your friend, what would you choose?

Q 2

If your friend's ex-boyfriend (or girlfriend) asked you out and you wanted to go, would you?

Q 3

If you and your friend both tried out for a team or a play and only one of you was chosen, what would be harder for you—if you were chosen or your friend?

Q 4

On a scale of 1 to 10, what kind of friend are you? What do you need to work on to be a better friend?

Q 5

What three qualities do you value most in a friend? (**Leader hint**: Some examples include loyalty, generosity, spiritual depth, common interests, fun to be with, good personality, popular, same musical tastes, et cetera.)

In your opinion,
what can break up
(or badly damage) a
friendship?

Do you have a
close friend of a
different race? What
challenges does this friendship present?

If a group of your friends were doing something you felt was
wrong, and they wanted you to join them, what would you
be more likely to do?

a. Tell them no and try talking them out of it
b. Tell them no and leave
c. Tell them no and stay anyway
d. Join them

Is it possible for a guy and a girl to be friends and not be
romantically involved? What are some benefits of male-female
friendships? Some challenges?

Is it hard for you to make friends? Why or why not?

If your best friend started blowing you off, how would you
handle it?

When you have a problem with a friend, do you usually go
straight to your friend to talk about it, or do you discuss it
with another friend first? What process would you prefer if a
friend had a problem with you?

Q 13

If your friend were in a relationship you believed was bad for him or her, would you say anything? If so, what?

Q 14

If you shared some private information with one of your good friends, and later learned your friend told someone else what you said, how would you respond?

Q 15

If you were in a group that started talking badly about one of your good friends, would you say anything? If so, what?

Q 16

Have you ever had a friend get you into trouble? If so, what happened? How did this incident affect your friendship?

Q 17

Do you have any close friends who are of a different religion? Does it put distance in your friendship? Why or why not?

Q 18

Of all your friends, who is the best influence on you? Why?

Q 19

If one of your friends were involved in some kind of destructive behavior, would you feel responsible to do something about it? Why or why not?

Q 20

Have you ever been jealous of a friend? How did that affect your friendship?

A Look at Scripture

If your group wants a more in-depth Bible study on friendship, read the story of David and Jonathan (1 Samuel 18-20) so your students can learn what good friendship really is. This story touches on jealousy, loyalty, family dysfunction, and putting the other person first.

Q 21

Read Proverbs 18:24. What do you suppose is the difference between a companion and a friend? What do you have more of—companions or friends?

Q 22

Proverbs 11:13 and James 4:11 warn us about something that can do great damage to friendships. Have you ever experienced this? If so, how did it affect your friendship?

Q 23

Look at Ecclesiastes 4:9-10. How do these verses relate to friendship? Can you recall a time in your life when two were better than one?

Q 24

In Acts 9:26-28, Paul is having trouble being accepted by the disciples until Barnabas comes alongside him. What does Barnabas do in these verses that makes him a good friend? Do you know anyone like Barnabas? Are you like Barnabas with your friends?

Q 25

Do you have a friendship that's not doing well? What does Matthew 5:23-24 say we are to do? Is there anyone to whom you can apply this passage? If so, when and how will you do it?

GETTING INTO TOPICS

FAMILY RELATIONSHIPS

Q 1

If you had to spend a week with one member of your family, who would you spend it with and why?

Q 2

Which family relationship are you happiest with? Which relationship is the most challenging? (**Leader hint**: siblings included!)

Q 3

How would you describe the perfect family?

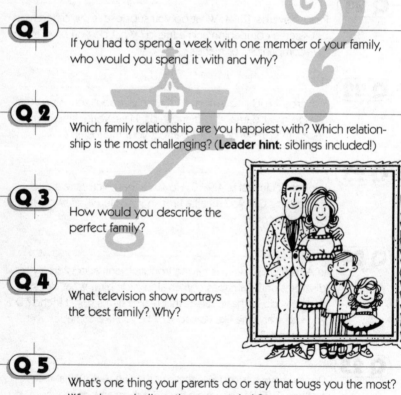

Q 4

What television show portrays the best family? Why?

Q 5

What's one thing your parents do or say that bugs you the most? Why do you believe they say or do it?

How much time (per day) do you spend communicating with your parents? What do you talk about the most?

What role do you play in your family?
a. the Peacemaker? (the one who makes sure everyone's okay)
b. the Caretaker? (the responsible one)
c. the Rebel? (the one who's always in trouble)
d. the Outcast? (the one who gets neglected or forgotten)

What do you wish you and your parent(s) talked about more often? Is there anything you wish you could talk about more openly with them?

Of all your friends, whose parents do you get along with the best? Why?

In your family, if you had to name the favorite child and the problem child, who would you name and why?

Do you or anyone you know live in a "blended family" (one family with children from previous marriages or relationships)? What are the challenges of being part of a blended family? Are there any benefits?

When parents get divorced, who (in your opinion) suffers the most—the kids, the mother, or the father? Why?

Should parents who want to divorce stay together for the sake of the children? Why or why not?

What do you think is the hardest thing about being raised by a single parent?

Who are you most like—your mom or your dad? In what ways?

How does your family deal with conflict? (e.g., talk openly, yell, walk away) If you could change the way your family communicates, what would you change?

Do you have any traditions in your family? If so, what's your favorite tradition? If not, what do you wish your family did together more often?

Is it hard or easy for you to respect your parent(s)? Why?

Is there something your parents do that you hope to never do yourself? If so, what is it?

Would you say parents have a strong influence on how their children turn out? Why or why not?

A Look at Scripture

For more in-depth Bible studies on family relationships, check out the following passages: Jacob and Esau (Genesis 27, 32, 33); Joseph and his family (Genesis 37, 42-45); Ruth and Naomi (Ruth 1); David and his brothers (1 Samuel 16-17). These passages explore all kinds of family dynamics and show how these Bible heroes wrestled with the same issues we wrestle with today!

What do you think it means to "honor" your parents? (Ephesians 6:2) What are some specific ways you could honor yours?

Look at Matthew 10:37. Are you able to put Christ ahead of your parents? Why or why not? Do they put Christ first in their lives?

Look at Proverbs 12:1. According to this verse, how should you respond to your parents' discipline? Is this difficult for you? Do you think the way kids are disciplined affects the way they turn out? If so, how?

Do you ever feel like your parents lecture you too much? Why do you think they do that? What does Proverbs 1:8-9 say about how you should respond to them? When is this the hardest for you?

In 2 Timothy 1:5, Paul tells Timothy how his mother and grandmother have influenced him spiritually. What sort of spiritual influence have your parents had on you? Your grandparents? What kind of spiritual influence do you have on your parents?

LOVE, SEX, AND DATING

Q 1

Which of the following kinds of love have you experienced?
a. "I love you for the way you look" (love based on looks)
b. "I love you for what you can do" (love based on admiration)
c. "I love you for the way you make me feel" (love based on magical feelings)
d. "I love you no matter what" (love that's unconditional)

Q 2

What three qualities do you find most attractive in a person of the opposite sex? Which quality is most important to you?

Q 3

Do you believe our culture's sexual standards are damaging to us in any way? Why or why not?

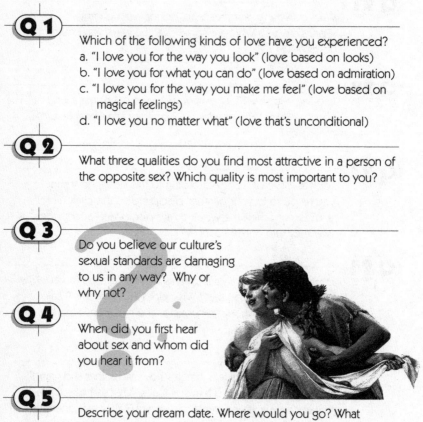

Q 4

When did you first hear about sex and whom did you hear it from?

Q 5

Describe your dream date. Where would you go? What would you do?

Q 6

How does the media portray falling in love? Do you believe the media's portrayal is accurate?

Q 7

If you were on a date and you had two hours, a half a tank of gas, and $5, what would you do on your date?

Q 8

If you could have any question answered about the opposite sex, what question would you ask?

Q 9

If you could have any question answered about sex, what question would you ask?

Q 10

Do you think it's realistic or possible to stay a virgin until marriage? What advice would you give someone who wants to save sex for marriage?

Q 11

Do any of your friends visit sex-related Web sites? Do you think it affects how they think (or behave) sexually?

Q 12

Do you believe the Internet is a good place to meet people of the opposite sex? Why or why not?

Q 13

What do you believe makes guys feel inadequate around girls?

Q 14

What do you believe makes girls feel inadequate around guys?

Q 15

What kind of impact has the Internet had on the way kids are exposed to sex? Do you think parents should be worried?

Q 16

If someone asked you "What does it mean to fall in love?" how would you answer?

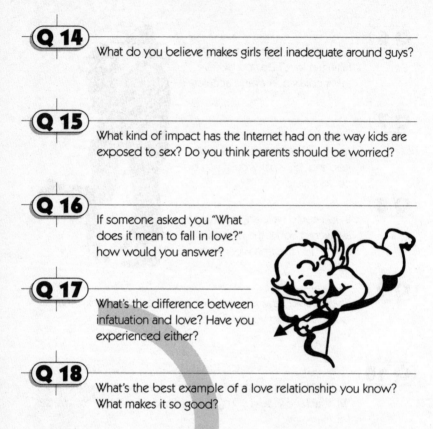

Q 17

What's the difference between infatuation and love? Have you experienced either?

Q 18

What's the best example of a love relationship you know? What makes it so good?

Q 19

Which fear do you think most frequently keeps people from having sex—contracting AIDS or contracting some other sexually transmitted disease? Why?

Q 20

Do you believe premarital sex has an impact on a person's future marriage? Why or why not?

A Look at Scripture

For a more in-depth study on love, sex, and dating, do a Bible study that compares the way Joseph handles temptation (Genesis 39) and the way David handles temptation (2 Samuel 11). Ask students what David does wrong and what Joseph does right—and how their stories can help us when we face sexual temptation.

Q 21

Look at 2 Corinthians 6:14. How do you think this verse applies to opposite-sex relationships? Does it only apply to marriage—or does it apply to dating, too? Is it okay for a Christian to date a non-Christian?

Q 22

What does 1 Corinthians 6:18-20 say about sex? How would you define "sexual immorality"? According to this passage, what might be some reasons not to have sex before marriage? What does it mean to "honor God with your body"?

Q 23

Look at Genesis 1:26-28. According to these verses, would you say God approves of sex or not? What does verse 28 say God did before he told them to "be fruitful and multiply"? Do you believe God gave sex as a blessing? Why didn't he choose some less pleasurable way for us to multiply? What does this tell you about God?

Q 24

Genesis 2:21-24 describes why God brought man and woman together. According to verse 24, what happens when a man and woman are united? According to this verse, do you believe God has created sex exclusively for marriage? Why or why not?

Q 25

What does 1 Thessalonians 4:3-6 say about sexual behavior? What are some reasons Paul gives for why we should learn to control our bodies? According to verse 6, what is another reason (besides our own purity) that we should control ourselves? Would you say that sex outside of marriage is something you give to someone, or something you take from that person?

MISSIONS AND SERVICE

Do you believe we have a responsibility to help the poor?

Do you believe rich people are
happier than poor people?
Why or why not?

Do you consider yourself rich or
poor? Why?

Where have you seen the most poverty? How did it affect you?

Have you ever been on a service project or mission trip to
minister to the poor or oppressed? If so, how did you feel
after it was over?

Q 6

Do you believe there is more contentment in making money or giving it away? Why?

Q 7

How would you define *materialism?* Do you think you are materialistic? Why or why not?

Q 8

Is it wrong for Christians to be wealthy? Why or why not?

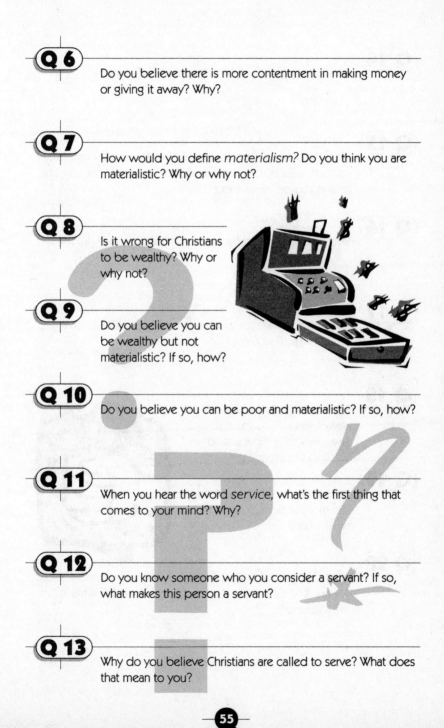

Q 9

Do you believe you can be wealthy but not materialistic? If so, how?

Q 10

Do you believe you can be poor and materialistic? If so, how?

Q 11

When you hear the word *service*, what's the first thing that comes to your mind? Why?

Q 12

Do you know someone who you consider a servant? If so, what makes this person a servant?

Q 13

Why do you believe Christians are called to serve? What does that mean to you?

Q 14

What are some ways to give besides giving money?

Q 15

What possessions do you consider necessities (things you can't do without)? What things do you consider luxuries (things you can do without)?

Q 16

Which of your necessities could be other people's luxuries?

Q 17

Is it wrong to have luxuries when other people are starving to death? Why or why not?

Q 18

If someone gave you a million dollars that you had to give away, whom or what would you give the money to?

Q 19

Does giving to others make you feel more of God's love? Why or why not?

Q 20

What do you think it means to be called to the mission field? Are any Christians not called to the mission field? What is "the mission field"?

A Look at Scripture

For more in-depth studies on missions and service, here are two suggestions: Matthew 25:31-46 (the parable of the sheep and the goats) is a correlation between how we treat the hungry and the poor and how we treat Jesus; Luke 10:25-37 (the parable of the Good Samaritan) is about what loving our neighbor really means.

Look at James 2:14-17. According to this passage, how does your service relate to your faith? Is it possible to have faith and not serve others? Why or why not?

In Matthew 6:1-4, what does Jesus say about the way we are to give? Do you know anyone who gives like this? Do you give like this? What makes it difficult to give this way?

Read 1 John 3:16-18. According to these verses, how does our service directly relate to how much of God's love is inside us? Do you feel convicted or inspired by this passage? What do you do when you see someone in need?

Look at Ecclesiastes 5:10-11. Do you agree with Solomon's statement about wealth? Why or why not? What reason does verse 11 give for why we should share our wealth with others?

In Luke 16:19-31, Jesus tells a story about the consequences of not sharing your wealth. What is your reaction to this story? Does it make you uncomfortable? If you had to summarize the lesson in this passage, what would you say?

TOUGH TOPICS

WARNING: The following questions address real-life issues that are sure to spur lively, controversial discussions. Before throwing these out to your group, do some preparation and think about how you'll deal with differing opinions—*especially how you'll follow up when the discussion is over.* These questions don't include specific Scriptures, so it might be a good idea to look up related verses before your group meets and have them handy as the discussion heats up. (And you may want to make sure it's okay with your supervisor or leadership board to ask these questions, too!)

 Q 1

Do you believe it's acceptable to watch R-rated movies? Why or why not?

Q 2

Do you believe parents should restrict their kids from certain Web sites or give them total freedom on the Internet?

 Q 3

Do you believe there's music that Christians shouldn't listen to? If so, what music? Are there any TV shows they shouldn't watch? If so, what shows?

 Q 4

Do you believe it's okay for Christians to have guns in their homes? Why or why not?

Q 5

Is it wrong for Christians to overeat? Why or why not?

Q 6

Is it okay for Christians to drink if they're of age? Why or why not?

Q 7

When (if ever) do you believe it's wrong for Christians to drink?

Q 8

Is it acceptable for Christians to smoke? Why or why not?

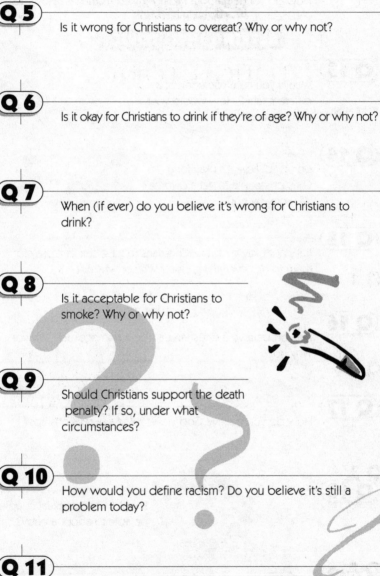

Q 9

Should Christians support the death penalty? If so, under what circumstances?

Q 10

How would you define racism? Do you believe it's still a problem today?

Q 11

Do you see evidence of racism in your school or in your friends? If so, in what ways?

Q 12

How do you feel about racially mixed marriages? How do you believe God views them?

Q 13

Would you date someone of a different race? How would your parents react?

Q 14

Do you believe it's okay for a Christian couple to get a divorce? Why or why not?

Q 15

If it's not okay for single Christians to have sex, is it okay for them to do "everything else"? Why or why not?

Q 16

Do you believe a Christian can be a homosexual? Why or why not?

Q 17

How do you believe God views same-sex relationships?

Q 18

Should a homosexual couple be able to adopt a baby?

Q 19

Does the Bible say homosexuality is wrong? If so, where?

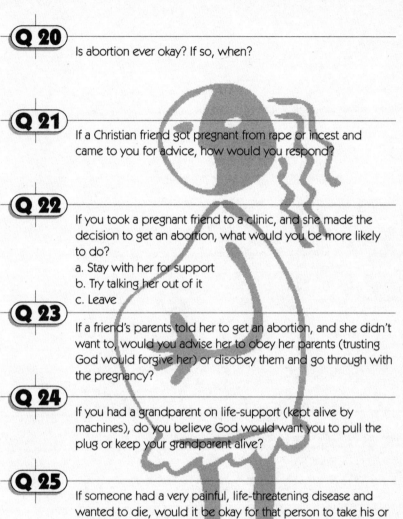

Q 20

Is abortion ever okay? If so, when?

Q 21

If a Christian friend got pregnant from rape or incest and came to you for advice, how would you respond?

Q 22

If you took a pregnant friend to a clinic, and she made the decision to get an abortion, what would you be more likely to do?
a. Stay with her for support
b. Try talking her out of it
c. Leave

Q 23

If a friend's parents told her to get an abortion, and she didn't want to, would you advise her to obey her parents (trusting God would forgive her) or disobey them and go through with the pregnancy?

Q 24

If you had a grandparent on life-support (kept alive by machines), do you believe God would want you to pull the plug or keep your grandparent alive?

Q 25

If someone had a very painful, life-threatening disease and wanted to die, would it be okay for that person to take his or her own life? Would you be willing to help that person die if asked?

GETTING INTO THE WORD

**30 Ready-to-Go
Bible studies**
(10 questions per study)
with Topical Focuses

4 FRIENDS
CARRYING YOUR FRIENDS TO JESUS *(MARK 2)*

DISCUSSION QUESTIONS

Have you ever brought a friend to a Christian event or retreat? If not, why not? If so, were you nervous or apprehensive? How did your friend respond?

If you had the power to bring anyone to Christ, what person would you choose? What keeps you from doing that?

OBSERVATION QUESTIONS

Read Mark 2:1-5. What does this passage say about Jesus' popularity at this time? Whose faith is Jesus impressed with?

Read Mark 2:6-8. What do these verses tell you about Jesus? Where in this passage does he prove he's more than just a teacher?

Read Mark 2:9-12. According to these verses, why does Jesus heal the paralytic? Who sees the healing? How do they respond?

INTERPRETATION QUESTIONS

In Mark 2:5, Jesus notices the faith of the paralytic's friends. What do they do that shows their great faith? What risks do they take by doing what they did?

In Mark 2:8, Jesus responds to the thoughts of the teachers of the law. Since they haven't said anything, how do you think they feel when he reads their minds? Do you think this changed their opinions about him? Why or why not?

Q 8

Read Mark 2:9-11 again. Do you believe Jesus is more concerned with the paralytic's spiritual healing or physical healing? What does this tell you about the way God works in our lives?

APPLICATION QUESTIONS

Q 9

If four of your best friends brought you to Jesus, what do you think he'd want to heal in you? What is keeping you from that healing?

Q 10

Is there an upcoming event to which you could invite a non-Christian friend? If so, what can you do to try to get your friend there?

JOHN THE BAPTIST
HE MUST INCREASE *(MATTHEW 3)*

DISCUSSION QUESTIONS

Who's the most passionate speaker you've ever heard? What response did this speaker get from listeners? How did you feel about the way the speaker came across?

If someone said you needed to repent, how would you react? What does the word repent mean to you?

OBSERVATION QUESTIONS

Read Matthew 3:1-6. How is John the Baptist described? According to this passage, is he popular with the people? What verse(s) show you this?

Read Matthew 3:7-10. How does John's tone change when he sees the Pharisees and the Sadducees? What warning does he give them?

Read Matthew 3:11-15. How does John describe the difference between his baptism and Jesus' baptism? In what ways do you see John putting himself beneath Christ in this passage?

INTERPRETATION QUESTIONS

Look at the description of John the Baptist in Matthew 3:4. If John came today and preached, how do you think people would respond? What do you think made people take him seriously?

Q 7

Luke 3:15 indicates that many people believed John might be the Christ. How tempting do you think it was for John to build his own following and not point to Jesus? What do you think helped him stay grounded in who he was? (**Leader hint**: Have students back up their answers with specific verses.)

Q 8

Look at Matthew 11:1-6. Why do you suppose John sends messengers to confirm Jesus' identity? What happens to John that might have made him wonder if Jesus really is the Christ? What encouragement does Jesus give to John in Matthew 11:6?

APPLICATION QUESTIONS

Have you ever been in the position of having to trust God when the circumstances made it difficult to trust him or when you were questioning him? How did you respond? What in this lesson encourages us to trust God in spite of our circumstances?

Q 10

In John 3:30, John the Baptist says he must decrease, and Jesus must increase. For John that meant going from celebrity status to a prison sentence—and eventually a bloody execution. How would you feel if you were in John's shoes? If your life took that turn, would you still follow God? Why or why not?

MARY AND MARTHA
GETTING YOUR PRIORITIES STRAIGHT *(LUKE 10)*

DISCUSSION QUESTIONS

Do you feel as though you do a lot of the work around the house? If so, how do you feel about it? If not, who in your family ends up doing it?

When you have a lot to do and someone stops by, do you say you're busy? Or do you talk and put off your chores for later? How do you feel when this happens?

OBSERVATION QUESTIONS

Q 3

Read Luke 10:38-39. Who opens their home to Jesus—Martha or Mary? What does Mary do when Jesus arrives?

Q 4

Read Luke 10:40. What distracts Martha when Jesus arrives? To whom does she speak about her frustrations?

Read Luke 10:41-42. According to Jesus, who makes the better choice? What reason does Jesus give for why Mary's choice is better?

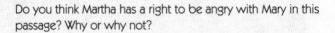

INTERPRETATION QUESTIONS

Do you think Martha has a right to be angry with Mary in this passage? Why or why not?

Why do you suppose Martha goes to Jesus with her complaint instead of talking to Mary? What does that tell you about the relationship between Martha and Jesus?

In verse 42, Jesus says, "only one thing is needed." What is that "one thing"?

APPLICATION QUESTIONS

Are you more like Mary or Martha? Why?

Does the way you spend your time accurately reflect your priorities? What "one thing" would Jesus say you need more or less of?

MARY

SAYING YES TO GOD *(LUKE 1)*

DISCUSSION QUESTIONS

If someone appeared in your room and claimed to be an angel with a message from God, what would it take for you to believe that statement?

If you learned you were pregnant (out of wedlock), what would be the most difficult thing to deal with—your parents' reactions, your friends' reactions, or your school's reaction? (**Leader hint**: for guys, you may want to ask a different question —*If your girlfriend told you she was pregnant, and you knew you weren't the father, how would you respond?*)

OBSERVATION QUESTIONS

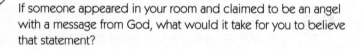

Read Luke 1:26-28. What do we know about Mary from these verses? What does the angel say to her?

Read Luke 1:29-33. What is Mary's first response to the angel? What does the angel say about the baby to be born?

Read Luke 1:34-38. What question does Mary ask?
Why do you think Mary finally believes the angel?

INTERPRETATION QUESTIONS

How do you think Mary was treated because of her "label"
(being pregnant out of wedlock)? How do you suppose this
affected her relationship with God?

Q 7

According to Matthew 1:19, after Joseph learned Mary was
pregnant, he decided to divorce her quietly. Do you think Mary
questioned God at that point? How would you have felt if you
were Mary?

Q 8

Look at Luke 2:39-45. How do you think Mary felt about
Elizabeth's response? What does this tell you about the way
God works?

APPLICATION QUESTIONS

Q 9

In Luke 1:37, the angel says, "Nothing is impossible with God."
In what area of your life do you have the most trouble believing
this?

Q 10

Mary's song in Luke 1:46-55 shows that she believes God's work
through her will have far-reaching effects. Do you believe God
wants to work through all of us that way? How do you think
God wants to use you? (**Leader hint**: Let students reflect on this
and write down some specific things to which God may be
calling them.)

SAUL TO PAUL
CHANGED BY CHRIST *(ACTS 9)*

DISCUSSION QUESTIONS

Have you ever seen someone radically change after a conversion experience? If so, how did that person change? How did it affect that person's friends?

Q 2

Have you ever experienced an obvious, almost tangible presence of Christ in your life? If so, what happened as a result of your experience?

OBSERVATION QUESTIONS

Read Acts 9:1-6. How is Saul described before his encounter with Christ? What are the first words Jesus says to him? What does Saul call him when he answers?

Q 4

Read Acts 9:7-16. What do the men around Saul hear when he has his vision? What do they see? Whom does the Lord speak to besides Paul?

Read Acts 9:17-22. What happens to Saul when Ananias places his hands on him? How do people react when they see the change in Saul's life?

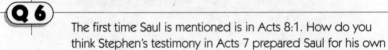

INTERPRETATION QUESTIONS

The first time Saul is mentioned is in Acts 8:1. How do you think Stephen's testimony in Acts 7 prepared Saul for his own conversion experience?

Look at Saul's encounter with Christ in Acts 9:4-8. Why do you think Saul calls him "Lord" before he knows who's speaking to him? (verse 4) Why do you suppose he's blinded for three days before Ananias is told to restore his sight?

Look at what the Lord says about Saul in Acts 9:15-16. What does this tell you about what it means to live the Christian life?

APPLICATION QUESTIONS

What changes in your life have occurred since you began your relationship with Christ? What changes do you think God still wants to make?

After his conversion, Paul was called to carry the message of Christ to the Gentiles. If someone asked you what God wanted to do through you, how would you respond? What might God be calling you to do? Whom might God be calling you to reach?

PETER
WALKING BY FAITH *(MATTHEW 14)*

DISCUSSION QUESTIONS

What's the scariest thing you've ever done? What made it scary? (**Leader hint**: If kids are stumped, it can be anything from speaking to a group of people, to rock climbing, to going on an amusement park ride, et cetera.)

Have you ever thought you saw (or felt) a ghost or some other-worldly force around you? If so, describe your experience.

OBSERVATION QUESTIONS

Read Matthew 14:22-24. Why are the disciples in the boat alone? Where does Jesus go?

Read Matthew 14:25-28. How do the disciples react when they see Jesus walking on the lake? How does Peter react? What is the difference between the two reactions?

Read Matthew 14:29-32. What causes Peter to begin sinking? What does Jesus do? How do the disciples respond to all they see?

INTERPRETATION QUESTIONS

Look at Matthew 14:22. What is Jesus' purpose in sending out his disciples by themselves?

How does Peter change between verse 28 and verse 30? What causes the change?

What's the difference between how the disciples experience Jesus and how Peter experiences Jesus? What are the differences between their faiths?

APPLICATION QUESTIONS

If you had to put yourself in this story, would your faith be more like Peter's or the disciples'? Why?

Q 10

Where in your life might God be leading you to "step out of the boat" and trust him? What could you do this week to take that first step?

PHILIP
SHARING THE FAITH *(ACTS 8:26-40)*

DISCUSSION QUESTIONS

 Q 1

What thoughts or images come to mind when you hear the word "evangelism"? What are some good and bad examples of evangelism you've observed?

Q 2

If someone said to you, "Explain to me what it means to be a Christian," what would you say? (**Leader hint**: Have two kids role-play—one sharing the Christian faith with the other.)

OBSERVATION QUESTIONS

Q 3

Read Acts 8:26-30. What leads Philip to go to the eunuch's chariot? What's the first thing he does? What's the first thing he says?

Q 4

Read Acts 8:31-35. What do you observe about Philip's approach? Who directs the conversation more—Philip or the eunuch?

Read Acts 8:36-39. What does the eunuch want to do after
Philip tells him about Jesus? What does he do after Philip leaves?

INTERPRETATION QUESTIONS

Look at Acts 8:26-30. What do these verses tell you about
Philip's relationship with God? How does Philip's relationship
with God affect the way he shares his faith?

Look at verse 30. What does Philip's approach tell you about
sharing your faith with others? What strategies does he use?

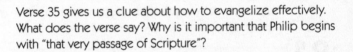

Verse 35 gives us a clue about how to evangelize effectively.
What does the verse say? Why is it important that Philip begins
with "that very passage of Scripture"?

APPLICATION QUESTIONS

Have you ever shared your faith with a friend? If so, how did it
go? If not, what has held you back?

If you had to write four tips on how to share your faith based
on Philip's example in this passage, what would you write? Can
you think of one person God might be calling you to share your
faith with? Based on what you've learned from Philip, what's
one thing you could do this week to start this process?
(**Leader hint**: Have students write names and strategies on
paper and keep them in their Bibles.)

THE WOMAN AT THE WELL
FACING THE TRUTH *(JOHN 4)*

DISCUSSION QUESTIONS

Have you ever felt like hiding because of something you were doing that you didn't want others to know about? In what ways did you hide? (**Leader hint**: Students don't have to share their secrets, just what they did to hide them.)

If you knew someone who could read your mind, would you want to be around that person? Why or why not? How would that person make you feel?

OBSERVATION QUESTIONS

Read John 4:1-9. Who speaks first—Jesus or the woman? What does the woman say that indicates her surprise that Jesus is speaking to her?

Read John 4:10-18. What is the difference between the water from the well and the kind of water Jesus offers? What does Jesus want from the woman before he gives her his water?

Q 5

Read John 4:19-26. What question does the woman ask about worship? How does Jesus answer her? What does he tell her about himself?

INTERPRETATION QUESTIONS

Q 6

Note what Jesus says about the way people are supposed to worship in verses 23 and 24. How does he demonstrate that to the woman in the way he confronts her?

Q 7

What does the woman say or do in this passage that shows how she feels about herself? What does Jesus say or do in this passage that shows how he feels about her? (**Leader hint**: You may want to divide students into pairs, have them write down their thoughts about the passage, and share them with the group.)

Q 8

Why do you think Jesus tells this woman he's the Messiah? As you look at what the woman does after her encounter with Jesus (verses 27-30, 39-42), what do you think was his ultimate purpose in causing her to face the truth about herself?

APPLICATION QUESTIONS

Q 9

Put yourself in this story. If you were at the well that day, what do you think Jesus would say to you? What would he want you to examine in your life?

Q 10

What are some things—besides God—that fulfill you? What are some steps you could take this week to let God alone quench your spiritual thirst?

STEPHEN
COURAGE IN ADVERSITY *(ACTS 6, 7)*

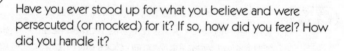

DISCUSSION QUESTIONS

Q1

Have you ever stood up for what you believe and were persecuted (or mocked) for it? If so, how did you feel? How did you handle it?

Q2

What thoughts or images come to mind when you hear the word "martyr"? Who is an example of a martyr?

OBSERVATION QUESTIONS

Q3

Read Acts 6:8-10. How is Stephen described in these verses? According to verse 10, what happens to people when they try to argue with him?

Q4

Read Acts 6:11-15. Why is Stephen brought before the Sanhedrin? What do they see when they look at him?

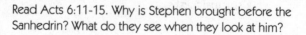

Q 5

Now read Acts 7. What does Stephen do when he's given a chance to speak to the Sanhedrin? What effect does this have on these elders? How does he respond when they stone him?

INTERPRETATION QUESTIONS

Q 6

Why do you think the elders and teachers of the law considered Stephen such a threat? What did he do to them?

Q 7

Why do you think Stephen says what he does when he's brought before the Sanhedrin? (Acts 7:2-53) Why doesn't he defend himself instead?

Q 8

Look at Acts 7:59-60. Do you see any similarities between Stephen and Jesus in these verses? If so, what are they? Why do you think it says Stephen "fell asleep" after he was stoned?

APPLICATION QUESTIONS

Q 9

On a scale of 1 to 10, how bold are you about speaking your faith? What steps could you take to be a better witness for God?

Q 10

Is there a person (or group of people) you wish you had the courage to share your faith with? If so, what could you do this week to begin that process?

THE HEMORRAGING WOMAN
DESPERATELY SEEKING HEALING *(MARK 5)*

DISCUSSION QUESTIONS

Do you believe God heals people? Have you ever prayed for healing?

Have you ever received attention when you didn't want it? If so, how did it feel? How did you handle it?

OBSERVATION QUESTIONS

Read Mark 5:21-24. Who approaches Jesus first in this passage? How does he approach Jesus? What does he want?

Read Mark 5:25-28. What's the condition of the woman who comes to see Jesus? Do you see any similarities between her need and Jairus' need? What is different about her approach?

Q 5

Read Mark 5:29-34. What makes Jesus notice someone had touched him? How do the disciples respond when he stops to find out who it is? What does the woman do?

INTERPRETATION QUESTIONS

Q 6

Why do you suppose the woman touched Jesus' garment instead of directly asking him to heal her?

Q 7

While Jesus stops to heal the woman and listens to her story, Jairus gets the news his daughter has died. Do you think Jairus might have been angry with Jesus? How do you think the woman felt? (**Leader hint**: Keep in mind that it probably took some time for Jesus to listen to this woman's story, perhaps delaying the healing of Jairus' daughter.)

Q 8

The woman is healed publicly (and instantly), and Jairus has to wait to receive his daughter's healing—yet both get more than they asked for. Do you think Jesus had a larger purpose than simply the healings? (**Leader hint**: If kids need more prompting here, have them think about the effect this had on the woman's self image and Jairus' faith.)

APPLICATION QUESTIONS

Q 9

In this passage we see two people receive healing, but not exactly the way they wanted it. What does that tell you about the way God works in our lives?

Q 10

If you had the opportunity to approach Jesus and ask him for anything, what would you ask for? Based on your observations of Jesus in this passage, how do you think he would respond?

THE RICH YOUNG RULER
LETTING GO *(MARK 10)*

DISCUSSION QUESTIONS

Of all your possessions, which would be the hardest to lose?
Why?

If God asked you to give up everything and be a missionary to
India, what would you say?

OBSERVATION QUESTIONS

Read Mark 10:17-19. What does the rich young ruler call Jesus
when he asks him his question? How does Jesus respond?

Read Mark 10:20-21. What do these verses say about how Jesus
felt toward the rich young ruler? What does Jesus ask him to do?

Q 5

Read Mark 10:22-27. Why does the rich young ruler go away sad? According to Jesus, is it possible for the rich to enter the kingdom of heaven? How?

INTERPRETATION QUESTIONS

Q 6

Why do you suppose Jesus says in verse 18 that "No one is good—except God alone"? Why would Jesus say that in response to the rich young ruler's question?

Q 7

How do verses 18, 24, and 27 relate to each other? Based on these verses, how would you explain the way to inherit eternal life?

Q 8

Look at verses 29 and 30. What do you think Jesus means when he says those who leave everything to follow him will receive a hundred times as much in this present age? Why does he include persecutions in the list of what we get when we follow him? (verse 30)

APPLICATION QUESTIONS

Q 9

If Jesus approached you like he did the rich young ruler, what would be the "one thing" that keeps you from fully following him?

Q 10

Which of these is hardest to give to God—your plans, your comforts, or your relationships? What specifically could you pray about giving to God in order to deepen your commitment?

THE WIDOW'S MITE
GIVING ALL YOU HAVE *(MARK 12)*

DISCUSSION QUESTIONS

When you get an allowance or make some money, what do you spend it on first? How much do you save? How much do you give away?

In your opinion, how much of what we "possess" should we give back to God? Does this only apply when we get a job and make money? Why or why not?

OBSERVATION QUESTIONS

Q3

Read Mark 12:41-42. What is Jesus doing in this passage? Who is he watching? What does he see?

Q4

Read Mark 12:43-44. Who, according to Jesus, puts the most in the temple treasury? Why?

According to Jesus in verse 44, what's the difference between how the rich people give and how the poor widow gives?

INTERPRETATION QUESTIONS

Why do you suppose Jesus watches people put their money in the offering? (verse 41)

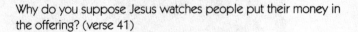

Why does Jesus say the widow put more into the treasury than all the others? Do you agree with him? Why or why not?

APPLICATION QUESTIONS

If you were to give like the widow, what would that mean for you?

How has your relationship with God impacted the way you spend your money?

What kind of offering do you think God wants from you? Can you think of anything besides money that you could offer to the youth group or church? What would it mean for you to follow the example of the widow?

THE WOMAN
CAUGHT IN ADULTERY
THE POWER OF GRACE *(JOHN 8)*

DISCUSSION QUESTIONS

 Q 1

Have you ever been the only one caught for something other people did also? If so, how did you feel? How did you respond? Have you ever gotten off the hook when someone else got caught? How did you feel then? How did you respond?

Q 2

Do you know anyone at your school with a reputation for something he or she did? Without naming names, how do people treat this person? How do you treat this person?

OBSERVATION QUESTIONS

Q 3

Read John 8:1-3. What was Jesus doing when the Pharisees brought the woman to him? What do they make her do?

Q 4

Read John 8:4-6. What question do the Pharisees ask Jesus? According to verse 6, what is their motivation? How does Jesus respond?

Read John 8:7-11. Does Jesus answer their question? What does his response cause the mob to do?

INTERPRETATION QUESTIONS

Look at verse 3. Why do you think the woman is the only one brought in? If the Pharisees are really concerned with justice, who else should have been brought there?

Q 7

Why do you think Jesus bends down to write on the ground? What does this do for the woman?

Q 8

Look at verse 9. Who leaves first as the people walk away? Why? How do you think the woman felt about Jesus after this experience?

APPLICATION QUESTIONS

Q 9

After reading this passage, how do you think Jesus responds to you when you sin? How would Jesus fill in the blank if he were to say to you, "Go and _____ no more"? (**Leader hint**: It may be a good idea for students answer this question privately —not verbally.)

Do you have a friend who has blown it (or has been caught in sin) and whom you could come alongside and help? What could you do this week to care for that person the way Jesus cared for this woman?

THOMAS

CONFRONTING YOUR DOUBTS *(JOHN 20)*

DISCUSSION QUESTIONS

If someone you trust tells you something hard to believe, are you more likely to believe your friend or find out for yourself?

When (if ever) did you come to believe in God? What evidence did you have to convince you God is real? If you don't believe in God yet, what evidence would you need to convince you?

OBSERVATION QUESTIONS

Read John 20:19-24. Where are the disciples when Jesus appears to them? Does he come through the door? Who's missing?

Q 4

Read John 20:25-26. What conditions does Thomas say must be met before he will believe Jesus is alive?

Read John 20:27-29. How does Thomas show his belief in Jesus? What does Jesus say to Thomas about his belief?

INTERPRETATION QUESTIONS

Look at verse 20. What similarities do you see between the way Jesus appears to the group of disciples and the way he appears to Thomas? (verse 27) What differences do you see?

Q 7

Do you think Jesus is angry with Thomas for not believing the disciples? Why or why not?

Look at verse 29. Why does Jesus say people are blessed when they believe without having seen? Does this mean he wants us to have blind faith? Why or why not?

APPLICATION QUESTIONS

Q 9

If someone asked you, "How can you believe in a God you haven't seen?" how would you answer?

What doubts or questions about your faith have you struggled with? What have you done to deal with those doubts? What could you do to find help in dealing with those doubts?

ZACCHAEUS
RESPONDING TO GOD'S LOVE *(LUKE 19)*

DISCUSSION QUESTIONS

Have you ever met (or been close to) someone famous? How did you act around that person? How did that person act around you?

Have you ever felt rejected (or talked about) by a group of people? If so, how did you handle it? If not, have you ever been a part of a group that did that to someone else?

OBSERVATION QUESTIONS

Read Luke 19:1-4. How would you describe Zacchaeus from these verses?

Read Luke 19:5-7. Who takes the initiative in their encounter—Jesus or Zacchaeus? How do the people around them react? Whom do they criticize?

Read Luke 19:8-11. What does Zacchaeus call Jesus? What two things does he tell Jesus he's going to do? What comes to Zacchaeus as a result?

INTERPRETATION QUESTIONS

In your opinion, whose reputation suffers the most in this passage—Jesus' or Zacchaeus'? Why?

In verse 10, Jesus says the Son of Man came to do two things. How does Jesus do both of these things in this passage?

APPLICATION QUESTIONS

Have you ever really felt God's love for you? If so, how?

How do you respond to God's love?

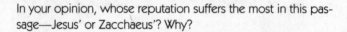

If you don't feel God's love, what is blocking you from feeling it?

AARON
BUCKLING UNDER PRESSURE *(EXODUS 32)*

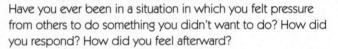

DISCUSSION QUESTIONS

Have you ever been in a situation in which you felt pressure from others to do something you didn't want to do? How did you respond? How did you feel afterward?

Name some examples of good leaders and bad leaders in our history. What was it that made them good or bad? Have you ever watched leaders make compromises? What was the result? Did people continue to respect them? (**Leader hint**: It may be good to think these questions through beforehand and have some examples of leaders—past or present—to get the ball rolling).

OBSERVATION QUESTIONS

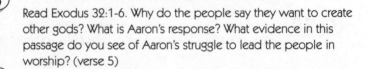

Read Exodus 32:1-6. Why do the people say they want to create other gods? What is Aaron's response? What evidence in this passage do you see of Aaron's struggle to lead the people in worship? (verse 5)

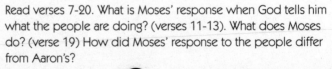

Read verses 7-20. What is Moses' response when God tells him what the people are doing? (verses 11-13). What does Moses do? (verse 19) How did Moses' response to the people differ from Aaron's?

Read verses 21-24. How does Aaron respond when Moses confronts him? Does he tell the truth? (**Leader hint**: Have students compare verse 4 with verse 24.)

INTERPRETATION QUESTIONS

Look at Exodus 32:1. What feelings or circumstances lead the Israelites toward the desire to worship other gods? What are some other gods we worship when we feel God is absent from us—or not doing what we want him to do? (**Leader hint**: A "god" is anything we go to in place of God to meet our needs—e.g., money, sex, drugs, entertainment, food, alcohol, et cetera.)

As you look over this chapter, compare Aaron's leadership with Moses' leadership. (**Leader hint**: As an optional writing exercise, have students write down all the things Aaron does as a leader and all the things Moses does as a leader and compare the two lists.) In what ways are they different?

Look at Exodus 32:21-22. Why do you suppose Aaron responded to Moses in the way he did? Can you understand why Aaron responded in this way? Have you ever been in a situation in which you've reinterpreted the truth to make yourself look better or avoid getting in trouble?

APPLICATION QUESTIONS

With what group or in what place is it the most difficult to stand firm in your values as a Christian? (e.g., school, sports, friends, family, work, et cetera.) How can you improve your ability to stand firm with that group or in that place?

Give an example of a "god" that sometimes takes God's place in your life? (**Leader hint**: Have students think of the things that occupy their thoughts and actions or the things they go to repeatedly for satisfaction and fulfillment.) What are some things you could do prevent that "god" from having control in your life?

ADAM AND EVE
TRUTH OR CONSEQUENCES *(GENESIS 2, 3)*

DISCUSSION QUESTIONS

Q 1

When you picture the Garden of Eden, what do you see? Of all the places you've visited (or have seen), which one most resembles your vision of Eden?

Q 2

How do you think the world would be different if there were no evil? How would your world be different? (e.g., your family, friends, school, et cetera)

OBSERVATION QUESTIONS

Q 3

Read Genesis 2:1-25. What is the first thing God says to Adam? What is the first thing God says about Adam? What are your observations about God based on his actions in Genesis 2? (**Leader hint**: Have students back up their observations with specific verses.)

Q 4

Read Genesis 3:1-6. What's the first question the serpent asks Adam and Eve? (verse 1) Who answers the question? (verse 2) Why does Eve eat the fruit? (verses 4 to 6) Why does Adam eat the fruit? Read Genesis 3:7-19 and list all the consequences of Adam and Eve's actions you can find in the passage.

The People Who Brought You this Book...
invite you to discover MORE valuable youth ministry resources.

Youth Specialties has three decades of experience working alongside Christian youth workers of just about every denomination and youth-serving organization. We're here to help you, whether you're brand new to youth ministry or a veteran, whether you're a volunteer or a career youth pastor. Each year we serve over 100,000 youth workers worldwide through our training seminars, conventions, magazines, resource products, and internet Web site (www.YouthSpecialties.com).

For FREE information about ways YS can help your youth ministry, complete and return this card.

Are you: ☐ A paid youth worker ☐ A volunteer   S=480001

Name_____

Church/Org._____

Address ☐ Church or ☐ Home _____

City _____State _____Zip _____

Daytime Phone Number (_____) _____

E-Mail _____

Denomination _____ Average Weekly Church Attendance _____

The People Who Brought You this Book...
invite you to discover MORE valuable youth ministry resources.

Youth Specialities has three decades of experience working alongside Christian youth workers of just about every denomination and youth-serving organization. We're here to help you, whether you're brand new to youth ministry or a veteran, whether you're a volunteer or a career youth pastor. Each year we serve over 100,000 youth workers worldwide through our training seminars, conventions, magazines, resource products, and internet Web site (www.YouthSpecialties.com).

For FREE information about ways YS can help your youth ministry, complete and return this card.

Are you: ☐ A paid youth worker ☐ A volunteer   S=480001

Name_____

Church/Org._____

Address ☐ Church or ☐ Home _____

City _____State _____Zip _____

Daytime Phone Number (_____) _____

E-Mail _____

Denomination _____ Average Weekly Church Attendance _____

||||

BUSINESS REPLY MAIL

FIRST-CLASS MAIL   PERMIT 268   HOLMES PA

POSTAGE WILL BE PAID BY ADDRESSEE

YOUTH SPECIALTIES
P.O. BOX 668
HOLMES, PA 19043-0668

I..oIIIdIudIIuuuIuIuIuIIIdIuuuIIuuuIIuuuIIdIuII

||||

BUSINESS REPLY MAIL

FIRST-CLASS MAIL   PERMIT 268   HOLMES PA

POSTAGE WILL BE PAID BY ADDRESSEE

YOUTH SPECIALTIES
P.O. BOX 668
HOLMES, PA 19043-0668

I..oIIIdIudIIuuuIuIuIuIIIdIuuuIIuuuIIuuuIIdIuII

INTERPRETATION QUESTIONS

How does God show his love for Adam in Genesis 2? What things does he do for him? Why do you think God set a boundary for Adam in verse 16? Was he trying to limit Adam's happiness or extend it?

What do you think the serpent's purpose was in asking the question in Genesis 3:1? What strategy does the serpent use to get Eve to disobey God? Why does Eve give some of the fruit to Adam right after she takes it herself?

Q 7

Why do Adam and Eve respond to God the way they do when he confronts them? What does this tell you about human nature when we get "caught"?

APPLICATION QUESTIONS

Q 8

What are some boundaries God sets for us that feel limiting, but are actually for our own good? (**Leader hint**: If students get stuck, have them think about the 10 commandments (Exodus 10), or some of Jesus' difficult teachings.)

Q 9

Think about the last time you were caught for something you did wrong. Did you deny it, blame someone else, or admit you did it? If it happened again, would you respond similarly or differently?

Q 10

When Adam and Eve sinned, they hid from God. Have you ever done that? On a scale of 1 to 10, how close (or far) do you feel from God right now? (1=far, 10=close) What would it take for you to move closer to God?

ESTHER
COURAGE TO STAND *(ESTHER 2-4)*

DISCUSSION QUESTIONS

If you knew for a fact that admitting you were a Christian meant you could lose your life, would you confess your faith? Why or why not?

Have you ever felt scared to do something you knew God wanted you to do? If so, what was it? Did you obey God or not?

OBSERVATION QUESTIONS

Q 3

Read Esther 2:1-18. Why is Esther brought to the palace? What does Mordecai instruct Esther not to reveal about herself when she arrives?

Q 4

Read Esther 3:1-9. What does Mordecai do to attract the attention of the royal officials? How does Haman respond? What decree does he want the king to pass?

Q 5

Read Esther 4:1-17. What does Mordecai ask Esther to do when he learns about the decree? What is her initial response? What does Mordecai say to compel her to take the risk?

INTERPRETATION QUESTIONS

Q 6

Look at Esther 2:7,17. Did Esther become queen because of something she was given or because of something she did? In what ways was God involved in her becoming queen?

Q 7

Look at the words of Mordecai in Esther 4:12-14.
Do you think it's fair for him to put Esther under such pressure? Why or why not?

Q 8

Before you look at Esther's response (verse 15), discuss all the options she has at this point in the story. Do you think it's her responsibility to respond the way she does? If you were in her place, do you think you would do the same thing?

APPLICATION QUESTIONS

Q 9

Do you let God use everything in your life for his glory? If not, what needs to change for this to happen?

Q 10

Make a list of all the things you've been given that you didn't earn or choose (e.g., family relationships, finances, talents, physical attributes, et cetera). Go through the list and write down how those things could be used if God had control of them instead of you.

GIDEON
THE BATTLE IS THE LORD'S *(JUDGES 6, 7)*

DISCUSSION QUESTIONS

Have you ever been called to do something you didn't feel qualified (or ready) to do? Did you do it? If so, how did you feel afterward?

What is the biggest "upset victory" you've seen? (**Leader hint**: It could be an election, sporting event, contest, et cetera.) What made it memorable?

OBSERVATION QUESTIONS

Read Judges 6:1-10. Why do the Israelites cry to the Lord for help in verse 7? How does the Lord respond?

Q 4

Read Judges 6:11-16. What's the first thing the angel says to Gideon? (verse 12) What does he ask Gideon to do? (verse 14) What reason does the angel give Gideon for why he'll be successful? (verse 16)

GETTING INTO THE WORD

Read Judges 6:17-40. Two times in this passage, Gideon asks God for a sign. What are the two signs God gives him? (verse 20 and 40)

INTERPRETATION QUESTIONS

Look at Judges 6:15-16. Given all the reasons why Gideon doesn't feel qualified to be a leader, why do you think God chooses him? What does that tell you about the way God works?

Why do you think Gideon asks God twice for signs? Do you think this angers God? Why or why not?

Read Judges 7:1-21. How do the events in chapter 6 prepare Gideon for the events in chapter 7? Does Gideon seem less confident, more confident, or the same? Why do you think God pares down the army so small before leading it to battle?

APPLICATION QUESTIONS

What is the biggest battle in your life right now? What makes it difficult? What encouragement can you get from this passage?

Have you ever done anything in your life that you could not have done without God's help? If so, what effect has this had on your faith? If not, what effect has this had on your faith?

HANNAH

THE POWER OF PRAYER *(1 SAMUEL 1, 2)*

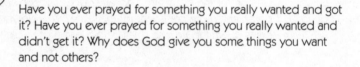

DISCUSSION QUESTIONS

In your opinion, does God always answer prayer? Why or why not?

Q2

Have you ever prayed for something you really wanted and got it? Have you ever prayed for something you really wanted and didn't get it? Why does God give you some things you want and not others?

OBSERVATION QUESTIONS

Q3

Read 1 Samuel 1:1-9. Describe the relationships between Hannah, Elkanah, and Peninnah based on this passage. Where do you see love? Where do you see jealousy? (**Leader hint:** Have students back up their observations with specific verses.)

Q4

Read 1 Samuel 1:11-28. How would you describe Hannah's condition when she prays to the Lord? What does she ask? What does she promise to do if her prayer is answered?

Q 5

Read 1 Samuel 2:1-10. What observations do you make about Hannah's prayer? What does she say about herself? What does she say about God?

INTERPRETATION QUESTIONS

Q 6

Look at 1 Samuel 1:10. How does Hannah feel when she first comes to the Lord in prayer? Do you think it's okay for her to show God her bitterness? Why or why not?

Q 7

Look at 1 Samuel 1:18. What does this verse say about the way Hannah feels after she prays and receives her blessing from Eli? What does this tell you about her trust in God?

Q 8

After Hannah fulfills her promise and takes Samuel to the house of the Lord, what does God do for her? (1 Samuel 2:21) What does that tell you about the way God works in our lives?

APPLICATION QUESTIONS

Q 9

In 1 Samuel 1:27-28, Hannah gives back to the Lord what he gives to her. Have you ever given back something to God that you've prayed for? If so, what?

Q 10

In 1 Samuel 2:1-10, Hannah praises God for all the things he has done. For the next month, keep a prayer journal and list all the things God does in your life. At the end of the month, share it with your group and have a time of praise to thank God for all his blessings. (**Leader hint**: If your group meets weekly, feel free to keep one journal for the whole group and log in each week.)

JOB AND HIS WIFE
THE TEST OF ADVERSITY *(JOB 1-2)*

DISCUSSION QUESTIONS

Some say all suffering is God's punishment. Do you agree with this statement? Why or why not?

Share about the time in your life when you suffered the most. How did you feel about God during this time?

OBSERVATION QUESTIONS

Read Job 1:1-5. How would you describe Job's character based on these verses?

Read Job 1:6-22. According to these verses, why is Job selected for Satan's test? What are all the things that happen to Job? How does he respond?

Read Job 2:1-10. How does the response of Job's wife differ from Job's? Of all the things that happen to Job, which hardships have an impact on her? How does Job respond to her?

INTERPRETATION QUESTIONS

Look at Job 1:6-12. According to this passage, what does Job do to deserve all the bad things that happen to him? How does that make you feel about God?

Look specifically at Job 1:9-10. What does this tell you about the way Satan works? What do you think Satan's goal is with Job? What is God's?

Look at Job 2:9. Do you suppose Job's wife has a good reason for being so bitter? What is the biggest difference between Job's faith and his wife's faith?

APPLICATION QUESTIONS

Q 9

Is your faith more like Job's or his wife's? On a scale of 1 to 10, 1 being Job's wife's faith and 10 being Job's, where would you put yourself? Why?

Q 10

Look at Job 1:21 and Job 2:10. What reasons does Job give us for accepting whatever circumstances come our way? Is this how you live your life? How would your attitude change about your circumstances if you applied this lesson to your life right now?

JOSEPH AND POTIPHAR'S WIFE

TACKLING TEMPTATION *(GENESIS 39)*

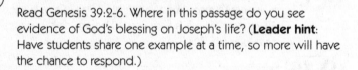

DISCUSSION QUESTIONS

Q 1

What temptation is hardest for you to deal with as a Christian? What force makes it difficult—your desires or pressure from others?

Q 2

If someone said, "Give me three things I can do to help me avoid sinning when I am tempted," how would you advise that person?

OBSERVATION QUESTIONS

Q 3

Read Genesis 39:2-6. Where in this passage do you see evidence of God's blessing on Joseph's life? (**Leader hint**: Have students share one example at a time, so more will have the chance to respond.)

Q 4

Go through Genesis 39:7-12 and make a list of all the things Joseph does in this passage to combat temptation. (**Leader hint**: This would be a good writing exercise for students individually or in pairs.)

Look at Genesis 39:2-6 and verses 20-23. What similarities do you see in these two passages? As you read the verses, pick out words or phrases you find in both. How are the two scenes different? How are they the same?

INTERPRETATION QUESTIONS

Read through Genesis 39:6-12 again and list all the circumstances that lead to Joseph's temptation. Of these circumstances, which are under his control? Which are not? What does that tell you about temptation?

Read Genesis 39:13-20. Why do you suppose Potiphar's wife lies about Joseph and has him thrown in jail? Why do you think Potiphar believes her? How do you think Joseph feels when he ends up in jail?

How does God take care of Joseph during and after his temptation? (verses 21-23) Do you think God does enough to show Joseph he loves him? Why or why not?

APPLICATION QUESTIONS

What do you notice about the way Joseph handles his temptation that you could apply to your life?

Write down any temptation(s) you're facing right now that are difficult for you to handle. Next to each, write down a strategy Joseph used that could help you with that particular temptation. (**Leader hint**: Appoint prayer partners to pray for each other and hold each other accountable.)

MOSES
CALLED TO TRUST *(EXODUS 3)*

DISCUSSION QUESTIONS

Have you ever heard God speak to you? If so, when? Was it an audible voice? What did God say?

What are some of the ways God communicates to people? Which one(s) have you experienced?

OBSERVATION QUESTIONS

Read Exodus 3:1-6. List all the things that happen in this passage that could be classified as "supernatural" (i.e., hard to explain or believe).

Read Exodus 3:7-14. What do you notice about God in this passage? What do his words reveal about his character? (**Leader hint**: Have students back up their observations with specific verses.)

What do you notice about Moses in Exodus 3:1-14? What do his actions and/or words tell you about him?

INTERPRETATION QUESTIONS

Why do you think God communicates with Moses in such an unusual way? What impact do you think this method of communicating has on Moses' faith?

Why didn't God call Moses to lead his people out of Egypt while Moses was a prince in Pharoah's palace?

Why do you think God waits until Moses is a shepherd in the desert? (**Leader hint**: If your group needs some prompting, tell them to think about the potential lessons Moses may have learned while he was tending large herds of sheep in the wilderness.)

APPLICATION QUESTIONS

Q 9

After his encounter with the burning bush, Moses responds with excuses for why he doesn't think he can do what God is asking him to do. Have you ever made excuses to God? If so, what were they?

Q 10

Do you feel like you trust God enough? If not, what are some obstacles that hinder your trust? (e.g., fears, insecurities, temptations, relationships) Write down your biggest obstacle on a sticky note and put it on your locker or mirror so you can pray about it each day.

NEHEMIAH
HEART FOR GOD *(NEHEMIAH 1, 2)*

DISCUSSION QUESTIONS

Q 1

When was the last time you heard some bad news? How did you respond? What did you do?

Q 2

When you hear about suffering in the lives of people you know, do you tend to stay away or try to do something to help? Why?

OBSERVATION QUESTIONS

Q 3

Read Nehemiah 1:1-10. What does Nehemiah do when he hears the news about his people? How does he start his prayer? What does he ask God for?

Q 4

Read Nehemiah 2:1-6. How does Nehemiah feel when the king asks him what's wrong? What does he ask the king permission to do? How does the king respond?

Q 5

Read Nehemiah 2:11-20. When Nehemiah sets out, to whom does he tell his plans? What does he do before he speaks to the people? How do the people respond? Is there any opposition?

INTERPRETATION QUESTIONS

Q 6

Look at Nehemiah 1:1-4. What do these verses tell you about Nehemiah? How would you describe him? How would you describe his relationship with God?

Q 7

Look at Nehemiah 2:1-8. What evidence do you see of God at work in Nehemiah's encounter with the king? Do you think the king's response (verse 8) is a result of God's work, Nehemiah's work, or both? Give reasons for your response.

Q 8

Look at Nehemiah 2:11-20. How does Nehemiah walk by faith in these verses? Who supports him? Who doesn't?

APPLICATION QUESTIONS

Q 9

When Nehemiah is faced with a challenge, he prays about it and then acts on it. Which of these two responses do you have the most trouble with—praying or acting? (**Leader hint**: If students have trouble with this, have them think about the last challenge they faced and how they responded to it.)

Q 10

Think of a challenge that faces you right now. What can you learn from Nehemiah's response and apply to that challenge? (**Leader hint**: If students can't think of anything, tell them to keep track over the next week of any challenge they face and next week share how they handled it.)

NOAH
FOOL FOR GOD *(GENESIS 6-9)*

DISCUSSION QUESTIONS

Q1

If you sensed God wanted you to do something that would make people laugh or ridicule you, do you think you'd be willing to do it? Why or why not?

Q2

Have you ever done anything that set you apart from the crowd? If so, how did it feel? If not, have you ever been around someone who did? How did that make you feel? (**Leader hint**: Your students may need some prompting here. Try to think of a personal illustration to get things going.)

OBSERVATION QUESTIONS

Q3

Read Genesis 6:5-8. What does this passage say about God? What does this passage say about mankind? What observations do you make about the way God views us from this passage?

Q4

Read Genesis 6:9-7:5. Write down all the verses that say anything about Noah. How is Noah described on the basis of these verses? How is Noah's relationship with God described?

Read Genesis 8:15-22. What's the first thing Noah does after the flood? What does God promise? What does Genesis 9:16 say will be the sign of God's promise?

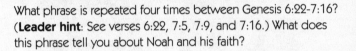

INTERPRETATION QUESTIONS

Q 6

What phrase is repeated four times between Genesis 6:22-7:16? (**Leader hint**: See verses 6:22, 7:5, 7:9, and 7:16.) What does this phrase tell you about Noah and his faith?

Q 7

According to Genesis 6:5-9, what makes Noah stand out from his generation? In what ways do you think his righteousness prepares him for what the Lord is going to ask him to do? (**Leader hint**: Noah was building character qualities that made him stand apart from the crowd *before* God called him to such an outrageous task. Our character and obedience is formed over time!)

Q 8

Look at Genesis 8:21. Does this verse indicate that there will be a change in human beings after the flood? God's promise is based on his word—not our behavior. What does this tell you about God's character?

APPLICATION QUESTIONS

Has God ever asked you to do something difficult or challenging? What was it? How did you respond? (**Leader hint**: It would be good for you to have a personal illustration ready—but let students take the lead.)

Make a list of all the ways your life shows others that you have a relationship with God. (**Leader hint**: Have pens and paper ready and have them be creative with this list!) Are you happy with your list? Is there anything God may be calling you to do that you aren't doing right now? If so, write it down and share it with one other person so you can pray about it together.

RUTH AND NAOMI

KEEPING COMMITMENTS *(RUTH 1)*

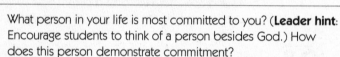

DISCUSSION QUESTIONS

Q 1

What person in your life is most committed to you? (**Leader hint**: Encourage students to think of a person besides God.) How does this person demonstrate commitment?

Q 2

What has been the most difficult commitment for you to keep? (**Leader hint**: This could be any commitment—to a person, a sports team, a job, a promise that was made, et cetera.) Why has it been so difficult to keep that commitment?

OBSERVATION QUESTIONS

Q 3

Read Ruth 1:1-9. Why does Naomi decide to leave Moab after living there for so many years? Why does she tell Ruth and Orpah not to go with her?

Q 4

Read Ruth 1:10-18. How is Orpah's response to Naomi similar to Ruth's? How is it different?

What is Naomi's first response to Ruth's commitment? (verse 15)
What causes Naomi to change? (verse 18)

INTERPRETATION QUESTIONS

Look at Ruth 1:8-14, 15-18. How would you compare Orpah's commitment to Naomi with Ruth's commitment to Naomi? Would you say Orpah is committed enough? Why or why not?

Why does Naomi keep trying to talk Ruth out of going with her? In what way does this show Naomi's love for Ruth?

Why do you suppose Ruth is so insistent on staying with and caring for Naomi? What is her motivation? Would you say this is a big sacrifice for Ruth? Why or why not?

APPLICATION QUESTIONS

On a scale of 1 to 10, how good are you at keeping your commitments? What makes keeping commitments difficult for you?

Think about the relationships you are committed to (either by obligation or choice). Which relationship is easiest for you to commit to? Which relationship is hardest for you to commit to? What can you do to show more commitment in your more difficult relationship?

SAMSON AND DELILAH
LOVE GONE BAD *(JUDGES 16)*

DISCUSSION QUESTIONS

Have you ever been in a relationship where you felt used? Without naming names or being too specific, what happened in the relationship to make you feel that way?

Think of the best relationship you know (or have seen) between a man and a woman. What are the qualities that make it good? Now think of the worst relationship you've seen. What are the qualities that make it bad? (**Leader hint**: The relationship can be real, like a couple the students know, or fictional, like a couple in a movie or a book. It may help to have some examples to reference.)

OBSERVATION QUESTIONS

Read Judges 16:1-3. What observations do you make about Samson from these verses?

Read Judges 16:4-14. What is Delilah promised if she learns Samson's secret? Does Samson tell her right away?

Read Judges 16:16-21. What is it that finally influences Samson to tell Delilah the truth? What happens as a result?

INTERPRETATION QUESTIONS

How do you think Samson and Delilah feel about each other based on their story in Judges 16:4-20? Would you say it's a relationship based on unconditional love? Why or why not? (**Leader hint**: Have students back up their opinions with specific verses.)

Q 7

Look at verses 6-15. Why do you suppose Samson lies three times to Delilah about how he got his strength? What does that tell you about their relationship?

Q 8

Do you think Samson knows the truth about Delilah? Why or why not? Why do you think he finally tells her the secret of his strength? Do you think he believes he can trust her?

APPLICATION QUESTIONS

What qualities do you value most in your relationships with the opposite sex? Does the relationship between Samson and Delilah contain any of these qualities? What is the most important lesson we learn from their story?

Do you have any relationship(s) that could be in danger of taking away your spiritual strength? Make a list of the relationships you have that push you closer to God and the relationships you have that push you farther from God. (**Leader hint**: It might be a good idea to have handouts with two columns available and make this a reflective exercise.)

SAMUEL AND DAVID
INSIDE CHOICE *(1 SAMUEL 16)*

DISCUSSION QUESTIONS

Were you ever chosen first (or toward the beginning) for a team? How did it feel? Were you ever chosen last (or near the end) for a team? How did that feel?

As a group, list the qualities that make someone a leader (or "on top" in our society). What are some examples of leaders in different fields in our world today?

OBSERVATION QUESTIONS

Read 1 Samuel 16:1-5. What does God tell Samuel to do? Where does God send him? What is Samuel's response?

Read 1 Samuel 16:6-7. What does Samuel think when he meets Eliab? How does the Lord respond? According to verse 7, how do people and God differ when it comes to judgment?

Q 5

Read 1 Samuel 16:8-12. Does Jesse have all his sons pass before Samuel? Whom does he leave out? For what reason?

INTERPRETATION QUESTIONS

Q 6

In verse 1, the Lord sends Samuel to Jesse's house to anoint the next king. What is significant about that? Before you answer, read Isaiah 11:1.

Q 7

Why do you suppose God chooses the least likely of all the brothers to be king? What does this tell you about God?

Q 8

In choosing David, God not only sets up an earthly kingdom, he paves the way for a heavenly kingdom. How is God doing that? Before you answer, read Isaiah 9:6-7.

APPLICATION QUESTIONS

Q 9

What are some ways God has demonstrated that he's chosen you? (**Leader hint**: Have students think about how they became Christians, or how they ended up at your group, in a church, in a Christian family, with Christian friends, et cetera.)

 Q 10

What are some things God might want to use you to do?

SOLOMON
THE EMPTINESS OF THINGS *(ECCLESIASTES)*

DISCUSSION QUESTIONS

Have you ever wanted something really badly, got it, and then realized it wasn't as great as you thought? What did you learn from that experience?

If you had your choice of having all the money you wanted, all the dates you wanted, or all the vacations you wanted, which do you think would make you the happiest? Why?

OBSERVATION QUESTIONS

Read Ecclesiastes 2:1-11. What are all the things Solomon does to find meaning and happiness? Does he find it?

Look up the following verses: Ecclesiastes 5:10; 5:11; 5:15, and 6:7. What does each say about seeking satisfaction on earth?

Read Ecclesiastes 12:9-14. What is Solomon's conclusion about the meaning of life?

INTERPRETATION QUESTIONS

Read Ecclesiastes 2:24-26. According to Solomon, what does pleasing God have to do with our happiness? Do you agree with him? Why or why not?

Look at Ecclesiastes 3:1-8. What is Solomon's purpose in describing life in this way?

Read Ecclesiastes 12:1-8. What advice does Solomon give to young people? Why do you think he gives this advice?

APPLICATION QUESTIONS

Q 9

How would you fill in the following sentence: *If I only had _____, I'd be happy.* Would having this thing keep you happy for very long? Why or why not?

Q 10

Of all the wisdom Solomon shared in the verses we've examined, what hits home the most? Why? What is something specific you can do right now to apply this to your life? (**Leader hint**: Encourage students to think about their goals, how they spend their time, et cetera.)

SHADRACH, MESHACH, AND ABEDNEGO
ALLEGIANCE TO GOD *(DANIEL 3)*

DISCUSSION QUESTIONS

Would you say you practice your faith more publicly or privately? What reasons do you have for living your faith that way?

If someone put a gun to your head and said, "You must deny Christ or die!" what would you do?

OBSERVATION QUESTIONS

Q3

Read Daniel 3:1-7. What do you notice about Nebuchadnezzar based on this passage? What do you notice about the people in his kingdom?

Q4

Read Daniel 3:8-18. Why do Shadrach, Meshach, and Abednego get into trouble? How do they demonstrate their confidence in God? Do they know God will rescue them?

Read Daniel 3:19-30. What happens when Shadrach, Meshach, and Abednego are thrown into the fire? Who dies? Who lives? How many people walk out of the fire?

INTERPRETATION QUESTIONS

Look at Daniel 3:16-18. Would you say Shadrach, Meshach, and Abednego's faith is based on the confidence that God would prove himself? Why or why not?

Look at Nebuchadnezzar's words and actions in verses 15, 19, and 28. What do these verses say about Nebuchadnezzar?

Why do you think God rescues Shadrach, Meshach, and Abednego? What do you think would have happened if he didn't?

APPLICATION QUESTIONS

What idols do people worship today? How do they worship them? (**Leader hint**: Be prepared with some suggestions if kids are stumped—e.g., popularity, sports, money, alcohol and drugs, sexual desire, et cetera.) Of all the idols you've encountered, which are you most tempted by? How can you avoid being tempted by that idol?

Would you say that God is first in your life? If so, how do you show that? If not, what would you have to give up or change in order for God to be first?

Resources from Youth Specialties

Ideas Library

Ideas Library on CD-ROM 2.0
Administration, Publicity, & Fundraising
Camps, Retreats, Missions, & Service Ideas
Creative Meetings, Bible Lessons, & Worship Ideas
Crowd Breakers & Mixers
Discussion & Lesson Starters
Discussion & Lesson Starters 2
Drama, Skits, & Sketches
Drama, Skits, & Sketches 2
Drama, Skits, & Sketches 3
Games
Games 2
Games 3
Holiday Ideas
Special Events

Bible Curricula

Creative Bible Lessons from the Old Testament
Creative Bible Lessons in 1 & 2 Corinthians
Creative Bible Lessons in Galatians and Philippians
Creative Bible Lessons in John
Creative Bible Lessons in Romans
Creative Bible Lessons on the Life of Christ
Creative Bible Lessons in Psalms
Downloading the Bible Kit
Wild Truth Bible Lessons
Wild Truth Bible Lessons 2
Wild Truth Bible Lessons—Pictures of God
Wild Truth Bible Lessons—Pictures of God 2

Topical Curricula

Creative Junior High Programs from A to Z, Vol. 1 (A-M)
Creative Junior High Programs from A to Z, Vol. 2 (N-Z)
Girls: 10 Gutsy, God-Centered Sessions on Issues That Matter to Girls
Guys: 10 Fearless, Faith-Focused Sessions on Issues That Matter to Guys
Good Sex
Live the Life! Student Evangelism Training Kit
The Next Level Youth Leader's Kit
Roaring Lambs
So What Am I Gonna Do with My Life?
Student Leadership Training Manual
Student Underground
Talking the Walk
What Would Jesus Do? Youth Leader's Kit
Wild Truth Bible Lessons
Wild Truth Bible Lessons 2
Wild Truth Bible Lessons—Pictures of God
Wild Truth Bible Lessons—Pictures of God 2

Discussion Starters

Discussion & Lesson Starters (Ideas Library)
Discussion & Lesson Starters 2 (Ideas Library)
EdgeTV
Every Picture Tells a Story
Get 'Em Talking
Keep 'Em Talking!
High School TalkSheets—Updated!
More High School TalkSheets—Updated!
High School TalkSheets from Psalms and Proverbs—Updated!
Junior High-Middle School TalkSheets—Updated!
More Junior High-Middle School TalkSheets—Updated!
Junior High-Middle School TalkSheets from Psalms and Proverbs—
    Updated!
Real Kids: Short Cuts
Real Kids: The Real Deal—on Friendship, Loneliness, Racism, & Suicide
Real Kids: The Real Deal—on Sexual Choices, Family Matters, & Loss
Real Kids: The Real Deal—on Stressing Out, Addictive Behavior, Great
    Comebacks, & Violence
Real Kids: Word on the Street
Small Group Qs
Have You Ever...?
Unfinished Sentences
What If...?
Would You Rather...?

Drama Resources
Drama, Skits, & Sketches (Ideas Library)
Drama, Skits, & Sketches 2 (Ideas Library)
Drama, Skits, & Sketches 3 (Ideas Library)
Dramatic Pauses
Spontaneous Melodramas
Spontaneous Melodramas 2
Super Sketches for Youth Ministry

Game Resources
Games (Ideas Library)
Games 2 (Ideas Library)
Games 3 (Ideas Library)
Junior High Game Nights
More Junior High Game Nights
Play It!
Screen Play CD-ROM

Additional Programming Resources
(also see Discussion Starters)
Camps, Retreats, Missions, & Service Ideas (Ideas Library)
Creative Meetings, Bible Lessons, & Worship Ideas (Ideas Library)
Crowd Breakers & Mixers (Ideas Library)
Everyday Object Lessons
Great Fundraising Ideas for Youth Groups
More Great Fundraising Ideas for Youth Groups
Great Retreats for Youth Groups
Great Talk Outlines for Youth Ministry
Holiday Ideas (Ideas Library)
Incredible Questionnaires for Youth Ministry
Kickstarters
Memory Makers
Special Events (Ideas Library)
Videos That Teach
Videos That Teach 2
Worship Services for Youth Groups

Quick Question Books
Have You Ever...?
Small Group Qs
Unfinished Sentences
What If...?
Would You Rather...?

Videos & Video Curricula

Dynamic Communicators Workshop
EdgeTV
Live the Life! Student Evangelism Training Kit
Make 'Em Laugh!
Purpose-Driven™ Youth Ministry Training Kit
Real Kids: Short Cuts
Real Kids: The Real Deal—on Friendship, Loneliness, Racism, & Suicide
Real Kids: The Real Deal—on Sexual Choices, Family Matters, & Loss
Real Kids: The Real Deal—on Stressing Out, Addictive Behavior, Great
   Comebacks, & Violence
Real Kids: Word on the Street
Student Underground
Understanding Your Teenager Video Curriculum
Youth Ministry Outside the Lines

Especially for Junior High

Creative Junior High Programs from A to Z, Vol. 1 (A-M)
Creative Junior High Programs from A to Z, Vol. 2 (N-Z)
Junior High Game Nights
More Junior High Game Nights
Junior High-Middle School TalkSheets—Updated!
More Junior High-Middle School TalkSheets—Updated!
Junior High-Middle School TalkSheets from Psalms and Proverbs—
   Updated!
Wild Truth Journal for Junior Highers
Wild Truth Bible Lessons
Wild Truth Bible Lessons 2
Wild Truth Journal—Pictures of God
Wild Truth Bible Lessons—Pictures of God
Wild Truth Bible Lessons—Pictures of God 2

Student Resources

Downloading the Bible: A Rough Guide to the New Testament
Downloading the Bible: A Rough Guide to the Old Testament
Grow for It! Journal through the Scriptures
So What Am I Gonna Do with My Life?
Spiritual Challenge Journal: The Next Level
Teen Devotional Bible
What (Almost) Nobody Will Tell You about Sex
What Would Jesus Do? Spiritual Challenge Journal
Clip Art
Youth Group Activities (print)
Clip Art Library Version 2.0 (CD-ROM)

Digital Resources

Clip Art Library Version 2.0 (CD-ROM)
Great Talk Outlines for Youth Ministry
Hot Illustrations CD-ROM
Ideas Library on CD-ROM 2.0
Screen Play
Youth Ministry Management Tools

Professional Resources

Administration, Publicity, & Fundraising (Ideas Library)
Dynamic Communicators Workshop
Great Talk Outlines for Youth Ministry
Help! I'm a Junior High Youth Worker!
Help! I'm a Small-Group Leader!
Help! I'm a Sunday School Teacher!
Help! I'm an Urban Youth Worker!
Help! I'm a Volunteer Youth Worker!
Hot Illustrations for Youth Talks
More Hot Illustrations for Youth Talks
Still More Hot Illustrations for Youth Talks
Hot Illustrations for Youth Talks 4
How to Expand Your Youth Ministry
How to Speak to Youth...and Keep Them Awake at the Same Time
Junior High Ministry (Updated & Expanded)
Make 'Em Laugh!
The Ministry of Nurture
Postmodern Youth Ministry
Purpose-Driven™ Youth Ministry
Purpose-Driven™ Youth Ministry Training Kit
So That's Why I Keep Doing This!
Teaching the Bible Creatively
A Youth Ministry Crash Course
Youth Ministry Management Tools
The Youth Worker's Handbook to Family Ministry

Academic Resources

Four Views of Youth Ministry & the Church
Starting Right
Youth Ministry That Transforms